AF077931

THIS BOOK IS ABOUT THE STRENGTH OF AUTHENTIC LEADERSHIP WITHIN AND FROM ORGANIZATIONS THAT ORIGINATES FROM A DIFFERENT 'STATE OF MIND' IN A POST EGO CAPITALISTIC SOCIETY. PETER LEUHOF WANTS TO INCREASE THE INNER STRENGTH AND INVOLVEMENT WITHIN ORGANIZATIONS AND DECREASE THE FEAR AND DISINTEREST. HE STRONGLY BELIEVES IN THE PROFITS OF A NEW MUTUAL CORPORATE TRUST AND CREDIBILITY. IT'S SOON TIME FOR AN AUTHENTIC STATE OF ANOTHER MIND AS THE NEXT PHASE OF LEADERSHIP AND ECONOMIC PROSPERITY. LEUHOF EXPLORES THE CURRENT AND FUTURE WAY OF MANAGEMENT AND CO-OPERATION IN A PLAYFUL MANNER AND TANTALIZINGLY ELABORATES EVEN FURTHER IN SEARCH OF YOUR PERSONAL MOTIVES, CHOICES AND CORE VALUES. HE SKETCHES INEVITABLE VIEWS, IS IDEALISTIC IN A PLEASANT TONED DOWN MANNER AND OFFERS A LOT OF USEFUL BEHAVIOURAL TIPS FOR A NEW KIND OF LEADERSHIP. FOR MORE INFORMATION PLEASE VISIT: WWW.PETERLEUHOF.NL

"CORPORATE AUTHENTICITY
IS YOUR NUMBER 1 SUCCESS FACTOR"

"AUTHENTICITY IS FINALLY
TANGIBLE AND BECOMES VISIBLE"

ISBN 978-94-90940-03-4

DISCOVER YOUR
CORPORATE AUTHENTICITY

PETER LEUHOF

State of Another Mind

Discover your Corporate Authenticity

This book is about the strength of authentic leadership within and from organizations that originates from a different 'state of mind' in a post ego capitalistic society.

The Dutch author Peter Leuhof explores the current and future way of co-operation within organizations in a playful manner and tantalizingly elaborates even further in search of your personal motives, choices and core values. He sketches inevitable views, is idealistic in a toned down manner and offers a lot of useful behavioural tips for a new kind of leadership.

Peter Leuhof is self-employed within his own company PeterVanPeetzen since 1998 and has about 25 years worth of experience within the (international) business sector and the semi government with many marketing and communication disciplines, situations, campaigns and media.

PeterVanPeetzen Ltd. is an independent marketing and communication consultancy and production intermediary. From a strategic point of thinking clients are served a better positioning, profiling and presentation of their organization or services.
Keywords are: Corporate Authenticity and Corporate Presentation.

Colophon
Peetzen Communications Ltd. (Publisher)
Peter Leuhof (Author)
Internet: www.peterleuhof.nl
Cover design: Erwin Bik, Gouda
15 September 2010
ISBN: 978-94-90940-03-4

© 2010, Peter Leuhof. Published by Peetzen Communications Ltd. All rights reserved. This publication is protected by Copyright (article 16 copyright NL law 1912) and permission should be obtained from the publisher prior to any prohibited reproduction, storage in a retrieval system, or transmission in any form or by any means, electronic, mechanical, photocopying, recording or likewise.

Dedicated to Wilma (and Rachel, Gerlof, Lieke and Eric)

With special thanks to the musicians of Muse, Keane, Coldplay, Porcupine Tree and Placebo plus Bowie and Waters for their pleasant company during the many solitary writing hours.

Foreword

My sense of urgency is growing. I see a fight, which is taking place around us and inside us. It is a fight revolving around a coming system change in our Western society.

I'm counting on a peaceful change, by means of a 'reset' concerning the way we think, collaborate and the way we manage and lead people. I want this process of inevitable change to work out constructively, through cooperating differently within and between organizations. And not destructively, by way of the street, throwing stones, physical violence or sabotage. It is still possible.

This book aims to be a reflective collage and it aims to inspire you. I would like you, as a manager, leader, politician, entrepreneur or employee, to look, search, think and position yourself once again. The post-war economical, political and social system is under pressure. By all sorts of strategies and tricks 'the powers that be' persist and stall. Evolution is still possible, but the chance of a major collision, system shock or irrational eruptions is growing. It is high time for reconsideration. It's time for a new subservient cohabitation with a fresh perspective on co-operation, with more authentic people working in more authentic organizations. That is what we need, as a weary humanity. That will provide us with fresh energy and new happiness.

The structure of the book is in such a way, that we as individuals dare to first look inwards in our hearts and consciousness, before we are able to show and share our authentic beliefs and convictions to others. I explore our deepest motives, such as fear (chapter 2) and hope (chapter 3) in order to try and set us free from (economic) slavery while trying to learn to embrace true values, to trust and by serving others.

The reason why I consider this as a necessity is because of the inevitable decline of our present ego capitalist system. This system now enters a downward, final phase. The book begins describing the current situation of our decadent and economic Western world and societies (chapter 1). They will not last much longer this way. But what comes after this naked, hard, debt driven capitalism, in which we prospered the last decades? How can we find new values in order for us to work together and trade with each other again? Are we going to act differently? I believe it can happen, but only if we are able to accept and embrace a more authentic state of mind.

Embracing authenticity is to everyone's advantage because it has two important core revenues for all of mankind: more confidence (chapter 4) as well as credibility (chapter 5). Truly, that is what we need. I first explore those two turnovers (in order to stimulate your enthusiasm and motivate you to read on) before I switch to what authenticity actually means on a personal level (chapter 6) and how this translates into the leadership in an organization (chapter 7). That leadership requires new, authentic leaders (chapter 8) who manage with a new corporate attitude that is more vulnerable, honest, open and sociable for employees and all other relations. This attitude should also be shown in its marketing, mass communication and the changed style for mutual collaboration (chapter 9).

And so the circle closes: in order to let authenticity be heard and become visible to employees, residents or consumers, we need different leadership, from an authentic state of mind such as a CEO, Board or MT member. These leaders can only achieve this state of mind based on a new inner belief and shared faith, by pursuing new economic drives and relational values. This new inner, authentic conviction is only able to grow if we really dare to leave behind our individual self-centeredness and our ego motives and greed. It takes guts to let go a little and detach from old capitalistic drives. I assure you that once you abandon your selfishness, you will enrich yourself. Giving and sharing yields far more satisfaction than just taking or conquering. You'll receive status and authority as other people flourish and prosper. And yes, sometimes 'less' really means 'more'. Your true satisfaction will come by letting others succeed with passion. You will be admired because of who you are, not because of what you possess or have gathered. By accepting limits and guidance and by loosening control mechanisms, you'll allow others to be innovative, surpass their limits and create a more sustainable future for us to share with others.

This requires a new attitude towards work, a re-freshened system of values and a sincere look into each other's hearts, motives and values. The book reflects my personal opinion and conviction that if people can become more authentic, organizations and institutions can attain this as well them being the best place of assembly for a change of system. These two (people and organizations) are not that far apart from each other and can be compared to a certain level. The yield of authenticity (trust and credibility) can be translated from a personal to an organizational level. This will work. This must work. This shall work. With the help of a new generation of authentic leaders and their, by then reassessed moral compass.

Peter Leuhof, Waddinxveen, The Netherlands

Chapters

Introduction page 10

The Situation page 12
The gap is growing, A change of system, No points of view, Support, End times, Slavery, Revolution, Powerlessness, Shock, Resistance, New compass.

The Fear page 28
Free, Structures, Island, The future is Now, Expulsion, Dreaming out loud, Capitalism, Transition, Offer from authenticity, The answer, New Objectivity, Credibility, Enough is sufficient, Passion wins, Responsibility, Show your soul.

The Hope page 48
Positive, Faith, Hope scientific, Hell, What hope does, The 'hope theory', Mistakes, Action, False hope, Stimulus, Yes we can.

The Yield Factor: Trust page 63
Vulnerable, Interest, How trust can grow (again), Deeper, Slow and quick, Sorry, Removal, Performance, Consistent behaviour, Your own strength, Systems and procedures, Attainable, Splitting cells, 65, Letting go, The corporation, Human scale.

The Yield Factor: Credibility page 86
Pyramid, Same as trust?, Indispensable, Crucial points for credibility, Reputation, Credible brands, Changes, Need and necessity, Emotion, SME and self-employed, Favourable costs, Some have it..., ... Some don't, Integrity, Qualities.

Authenticity page 104
Desire for genuineness, Old world, Worldwide, Complacency, Believing and trusting, Externally or internally passionate, Strictly personal, Rewards, Alienation, Your own brand, Nice job?, To be, Tension, You and us.

Towards Corporate Authenticity page 121
Basic principles, Meaningful, For everyone, Benefits, Some facts, From abroad, Baloney?, The other side, Different mindset, Generation Z, Adjustments, The sender, Mental handles, Brands, Qualities, grow, ready to, Charity, Unique singularity, Trends, SRE and Durability, it lives and it works, heart plus head, Being happy, Personal contributions, Grateful, Kind, Optimistic, Accept, Facilitate creativity, Invest in contacts, Overregulation and tunnel vision, Celebrate the amazement, Spiritual, Stick to your trade, Present.

The New Manager page 155
Vision, From the heart, Doing the right thing, Characteristics, Motivate to affect, Rules for everyone, Appreciate and praise, Turn inwards, Speak authentic, Moral leadership, Servant leadership, Effects, Serving is universal, Male or female, New classification, Intuition, Tool, Built-in consultant, With love?, Sensitive, Spiritual, Religion/Relation, Motivating, Out of love!, Personal note

Authentic Communications   **page 180**

Origin, Intrinsic, Value driven attitude, Other accents, Use of language, Different 'Umfeld', The turnover, Sensitive example, Strategically issue, Organizing opinions, Manipulation, Mutuality, Commitment, Consistency, Peer pressure, Attractive, Authority, The clever shortage, Seducing, In conclusion.

Justification	**page 205**
About the author	**page 208**
Sources	**page 211**
Quotes	**page 216**

1.

Introduction

It was in the eighties of the last century that I was first confronted with the statement: 'change is the only constant'. This meant, in my mental framework those years, there had to be constant reorganization in order to increase productivity and keep the employees 100% sharp.

Flexibility was the new 'buzz word' and it became a form of art to turn threats into possibilities.
Early on in my career I underwent the personal meaning of that statement, when I unexpectedly became redundant. My feelings understood it better than my mind. Generally, it appeared to have the following meaning: your use is limited and your skills are no longer wanted here, therefore ... leave (with severance payment).

> *Learning without reflection is a waste, reflection without learning is dangerous (Confucius) .*

Emotionally, it felt like blow to my self-esteem. Because I gave the best of myself, serving the purpose and requirements of the corporation. One consequence was that I decided never to get so unconditionally involved again, so that it could not hurt me again.

I also came to see my efforts, time, abilities and intellect as an emotional medium of exchange. Salary alone was no longer enough for my full physical and intellectual involvement. Also my emotional commitment to the policy and leadership were only available if it was equal emotionally compensated by higher management.

And yet ... this limited, rational involvement and calculated trust still feels like a restraining handicap, a shortcoming for an optimal and fruitful relationship and as a loss of economical value. A loss in terms of personal innocence as well as a loss in terms of unity, community, credibility, reciprocity and mutual trust. During the past 25 years the aforementioned words again started to get -and are still getting- more meaning and true value to me.

There's nothing like rejection, to make you do an inventory of yourself (James L Burke)

2.

The Situation

There once was a time, a time when something really exciting was asked during a first acquaintance or a job interview, namely the inquiry after 'your personal drive'. You were expected to describe it in a single word or sentence.

What you said was not that important, but the fact that you were able to say something, was an advantage. If you weren't able to say anything or if you were too nuanced, it would be regarded as a weakness.

It was the catalyst for volatility and speed. It was the time of 'sound bites' and 'management by statement' or: 'by slogan'. A knack (and time, money and patience) for details and interest as a prerequisite for long lasting rational beauty and preservation of value seemed to have disappeared and was left solely to the domain of the free artists.
Within organizations this drive for efficiency and productivity translated itself in an increase of systems, regulations, controls, measurements, quantity, figures, facts, easy ordering from catalogues and less involvement and interest in the own identity,

shared passions and the care for the well being of people. Attention to the well being of employees was boarded out.

A new time, a new mission:
Act Locally-Think Community (Pleu)

A different characteristic that I can remember from my first period in paid employment was the feeling of solidarity in organizations originating from common language, shared jargon, codes and symbolism. These factors still play an important stringent role in a lot of companies every day. For middle and higher management, both the proper way of dressing and fluent use of the right jargon is necessary in order to attain status, survive the jungle politics and be taken seriously. We prefer to mix Dutch with English fillers and American business terms (unfortunately I've been heavily infected as well).

This quick and tough yuppie Dutch – English did not contribute to an enriched spirit or a purified state of mind – of the average Dutch manager and a closer bond with sensitive employees. The alienation from what we experience as familiar and reliable is growing and the distant behaviour because of the unfamiliar, impersonal and unpredictable responses to our habits and our acquired demeanour is increasing. It seems to keep pace with the social individuality, multicultural habituation and integration, prodigality (we will learn to enjoy!), beginning hedonism and (spiritual) 'depillarization' between Dutch religious groups (every denomination used to organise their own RTV channels, political parties, schools, trade unions, newspapers, churches etc, in so called 'social pillars' in the previous century).

The gap is growing

The consequence of this all is an increasing mental and factual state of insecurity and ignorance. This also results in alienation between management and employees within organizations and a decrease in mutual personal commitment. This seems only to have increased in 2010. Directors and CEO's of larger organization operate disconnected from their workforce, often only motivated to serve themselves and sometimes they even embark on organized raids through for instance, unrealistic bonus systems.

Macro economically speaking we – being ultra capitalists – are working hard to make the lowest underdeveloped rural communities our urban production stooges. After the Indians and now Chinese, there are no other societies anymore who lend themselves as production slaves for the global free trade and market forces. Indeed, even if we were to motivate another society to become urban civilized, our fractional monetary system is a drama gone out of control. It is solely based on debt, credit and fake promises and is reanimated in 2010 - 2012, paid by the citizens. While we still desperately continue blowing bubble after bubble in order to keep everything in the air by means of 'adjusting' numbers en masse and the managed manipulation of stock market prices. Greed, money and exercise of power are considered to be the root of all evil. However, this valuable insight does not translate itself into any other kind of behaviour by governments or bankers.

> *When a government is dependent upon bankers for money, they and not the leaders of the government control the situation, since the hand that gives is above the hand that takes. Money has no motherland; financiers are without patriotism and without decency; their sole object is gain (Napoleon Bonaparte).*

A change of system

Capitalism seems to have had it, in her current, post-war shape. At the moment, it is the national state that makes acquisitions in the financial sector. Her influence grows. The limit of free enterprise on a large(r) scale seems to be reached; the debt has become, literally as well as figurative, too big. The mountain ridges are incalculable and promises cannot be redeemed anymore. To quote Cicero before the Senate of Rome in 55BC: 'The budget should be balanced, the Treasury should be refilled, public debt should be reduced, the arrogance of officialdom should be tempered and controlled, and the assistance to foreign lands should be curtailed lest Rome become bankrupt. People must learn to work instead of living on public assistance'. What a striking resemblance to our Western society today.

The credit pyramid game is over. The loot for some, as well as the damage for many, is stifling. Competition and shortage have proven their irrelevance and too much damage has been done, too much expulsion; too many suffering has been manipulated and too much exploitation brought on too much misery. So what now? What now, after this era of ego capitalism? By now we also know that socialism and, before that, communism aren't exactly ideal systems either.

It is painful to hear politicians with a total lack of vision for the medium-term reading aloud their speeches. The people don't believe that politicians from The Hague, let alone from Europe, are here to serve their interest anymore. There isn't a lot of expertise gained from experience over there anymore, that knowledge and experience is bought. We have a civil service and interest lobby often lacking human compassion, sound reasoning and sober commonsense. They consist of regents and politicians without a substantive vision or mission.

> *Politics is supposed to be the second-oldest profession. I have come to realize that it bears a very close resemblance to the first.*
> *(Ronald Reagan)*

No points of view

The content expertise in government circles these days come from the outside, from scientific agencies, lobbyists or from the industry. They are becoming increasingly mixed. Take, for instance, the 'Military Industrial Complex' in the USA or the power and influence of oil and the pharmaceutical industries. Shallow fads, viewer ratings and perceptions based on media management rule the country. Not a single leader dares to make himself redundant or vulnerable for the greater good of his country or all of its inhabitants, let alone to apologize.

> *In the counsels of Government, we must guard against the acquisition of unwarranted influence, whether sought or unsought, by the Military Industrial Complex. The potential for the disastrous rise of misplaced power exists, and will persist. We must never let the weight of this combination endanger our liberties of democratic processes. We should take nothing for granted. Only an alert and knowledgeable citizenry can compel the proper meshing of the huge industrial and military machinery of defence with our peaceful methods and goals, so that security and liberty may prosper together.(Eisenhower, farewell speech 1961)*

In the meantime the middle managers and the civil servants battle to survive, stuck in between the board of directors and the working floor, between policy and implementation.

Their influence is based on even more process control, hired (justification) consultants and coming up with extra regulations and rules. For our own safety of course! After all, personal risk and mental suffering are there to be entirely regulated and banished. Every new accident or problem and every tragic event is transformed into a new set of prohibitions and rules.

Think of the installation of even more street camera's, up unto Full Compliance and Business Solvency2 regulations (dealing and the possibility of personal prosecution of the CEO if it all goes wrong). The detachment from these methodologies, processes and what is really of value in the practical everyday life increases. Practical attainability and sense of reality get snowed in.

Support

Total supervision and electronic monitoring provide a sense of protection. Freedom is exchanged for a sense of safety. 'But you have nothing to hide, right?' is the misleading question and the manipulating coercion argument. There are more and more inhabitants losing the nerve to be a role model or dare to show a sense of empathy in order to help others. On the street we are quiet, shuffle past each other and only mind our own affairs.

> *You can have power over people as long as you*
> *don't take everything away from them.*
> *But when you've robbed a man of everything,*
> *he's no longer in your power (A. Solzhenitsyn)*

In small rooms and old churches without churchgoers on Sunday, we listen breathlessly to those few esoteric men or women, who share the path of their life and indicate that they found their personal eureka, going through deep emotional valleys and by keeping distance to the real world.

This interest in finding yourself, by setting yourself free from 'the system', is an amazing phenomenon. Because In the Christian tradition we already have been told for decades that 'we are in this world, but not from this world'. Anyway, who still undergoes the guidelines from 'The Holy Word' on Sunday voluntarily in these times of secularization?

Furthermore, children are hurt by divorces and a lack of constructive correction of their behaviour. We often spend more time on the purchase of a new car than on preparing for our child. And let's be honest, what is worth more with regard to receiving responsibility and achieving results on this planet? Still we want to spend less and less time on their (spiritual) upbringing and would rather work for a materialistic goal, whether forced by circumstances or not. Woe to the decadent society, that values this economical slavery more than attentive and present parenting; that stimulates individual enrichment above care for the weak.

End times
There is factual information available everywhere proving the increase of egocentric behaviour and the pure self-centeredness In cooperation, management, motivation, living together and the care for our offspring and elderly. Nothing completely makes sense anymore and nothing and no one is entirely believed. The distrust is massive, whether it concerns conspiracy theories (that 9/11 isn't what it seems, is pretty obvious to everyone right now), the NWO world government, the secret societies, pandemics, environmental lobby or old religious norms... everything that (and everyone who) points at a clear direction, immediately gets a public counter-argument.

Expertise is from, for and by everyone and vulnerability is mainly the concern of someone else or the problem of the government.

Discovering the true meaning of life and attaining self-knowledge have once again becomes a quest. The level of democracy in the relatively 'free' Western countries is declining. Privacy barely exists anymore. Freedom of speech, religion, education, travel and safety in general are under pressure.

> *The very word "secrecy" is repugnant in a free and open society; and we are as a people inherently and historically opposed to secret societies, to secretoaths and to secret proceedings. We decided long ago that the dangers of excessive and unwarranted concealment of pertinent facts far outweighed the dangers, which are cited to justify it. Even today, there is little value in opposing the threat of a closed society by imitating its arbitrary restrictions. Even today, there is little value in insuring the survival of our nation if our traditions do not survive with it. And there is very grave danger that an announced need for increased security will be seized upon by those anxious to expand its meaning to the very limits of official censorship and concealment. That I do not intend to permit to the extent that it is in my control.*
> *(JF Kennedy)*

For example: are all of the employees in your company photographed and provided with a pass already? Are their entrance gates, iris scanners, thumb scanners and is the company security force watching along? Exactly the fact that we believe that the threats from outside are actually real and that there is no alternative (so they say), robs us of all of our liberties.

Slavery

We still accept the saying: trust is good, verification is better. And for some people that really works out well. For numerical calculation, factual analysis, tuning equipment and machines ... constant verification is the best parameter to make sure things are functioning optimally. For a lot of citizens, professionals and employees however, control and verification are suffocating principles. And for an even larger number of people it robs them of the chance to grow towards their own authenticity and the pleasure to be allowed to make mistakes. Risk reduction and rational analysis are at the base of enterprises and of complex control systems. They often turn out to only provide a pseudo-security.

For the human mind is always capable of avoiding controls, rules, regulations and supervision and undermine them (e.g. consider the creative banking products 2008 - present). In our seemingly doable Western society everything can be arranged and organized and we no longer accept a single discomfort or personal suffering. Or so it seems. That is, however, not the truth. We are moving towards a boiling point of decadence, social engineering and make ability and therefore: a turning point.

> *There are three ways of dealing with difference:*
> *domination, compromise, and integration.*
> *By domination only one side gets what it wants;*
> *by compromise neither side gets what it wants;*
> *by integration we find a way by which both sides*
> *may get what they wish. (Mary Parker Follett)*

Revolution

The idea of reaching a turning point corresponds to the familiar thesis that time and events do not occur linear but in cycles or waves and that history repeats itself (although I think this is only happening at the exact time that history is forgotten).

According to the Maya's, a new era (of enlightenment?) will begin in 2012. According to Kondratieff (Russian economist until 1938, who thought of cycles as seasons), we find ourselves in an economic winter, with a necessary round of reorganizations in view due to the massive amounts of debts and uncovered promises and IOU's, amounting up to 605 trillion in 2009 already (BIS, 2/2010) and which are still increasing daily. Does this mean a period of hyperinflation or stagflation will come or will it become a 'Weimar '23 revisited' event?

> *It takes a lot of courage to release the familiar*
> *and seemingly secure, to embrace the new.*
> *But there is no real security in what is no longer*
> *meaningful. (Alan Cohen)*

According to the Bible we already are living in the End Times including all the foretold disasters on our moaning planet, haunted by destruction and misery. Think of the increase in earthquakes, hurricanes, disasters, volcano eruptions, wars and rumours of wars. In the same End Times the Islamic world expects the coming of the second Mahdi. According to the cycles of Strauss and Howe we find ourselves in the 4th turning point, heading for 'Crisis' (with after that a new 'High'). Cynics believe a dying imperial power like the USA/NATO combination, is only benefitted by a next world war outside of its borders, to avoid one domestically.

Getting the right, positive perspective in these startling times proves to be quite difficult. Our newspapers and TV channels are bursting with misery, violence, lies, failure, threats and pessimism. What do we teach our children to hope for -besides the next 'electronic gadget'- with such negative and poisoned?

information bombardments every day? Even the biggest optimist, believer, inspired or enlightened spirit gets numb and fatalistic and starts to wonder what's the point and what should come of this world.

Powerlessness

The frustrating thing about all of this is that our governments cannot or will not tell us honestly, how to translate this negative state of mind (only bad news sells) into credible or suitable legislation and measures. Without saying we embrace a sort of unrealistic, sacred common belief that humanity is indeed able to turn the tide of history, that we can bend the downward cycles someday soon. That optimistic belief will turn out to be false, for we will get our share of misery. Especially when the current economic crises will become worse and harmful to many.

Fundamental measures are not taken and proper adjustments to counterattack the structural problems, the wretched way of banking and reducing the mountains of debt, aren't made.

On the contrary.

We all continue the way we always did and hog level of debt are tackled by making even more debt, or moving the debt around together with even more rules and new monitoring regulations. Debt will not be reduced by more debt. If this goes on just a little while longer, no one will get the chance to oversee, organize, facilitate or lead the coming clean up calmly and wisely.

Shock

The chance that the economic change will not go by peacefully and evolutionary, but instead will feature a deep shock, is getting greater with every delay (all we do is shove the problem away to someone else: from banks to companies to governments to citizens to ... etc.). A recent example of a shock is for instance the economic crash in Argentina (2002), where the citizens became the victim of capital manipulation. People couldn't get access to their savings anymore and bankruptcies, revolts, hunger and a lot of personal misery happened while bartering, recycling and street trade became very normal again.

A more recent example is the situation in Zimbabwe where the political and economic crisis coincided with hyperinflation. There's hardly room on the banknotes anymore to print new zeros. In December 2008 a new note of 10 billion Zimbabwean dollars made its appearance. Prices doubled every day in that period, and the inflation was by far the highest in the world. In the end they embraced the US dollar, which will become a risky choice again. I would rather that we wouldn't reform like that over here, but instead come to our senses more gradually. While we still can.

> *When you come to the end of your rope,*
> *tie a knot and hang on. (FD Roosevelt)*

Alexander F. Tytler believer that greater civilizations developed themselves through a number of phases:
1. From bonding to spiritual faith
2. From spiritual faith to great courage
3. From courage to liberty
4. From liberty to abundance
5. From abundance to complacency
6. From complacency to apathy
7. From apathy to dependence
8. From dependence back into bonding

We are, according to my estimation anno 2010, in the transition from phase 6 to phase 7 and maybe even from phase 7 to phase 8.

Resistance

Already becoming gloomy from this small summary of misery? Just like me sometimes? Than grab the first possibility within your reach to make a small difference. The part or task close by, that you can still overlook, and begin to fight the general mood of gloom and doom. Every small action and peaceful deed in order to help someone is of great value. Remember that it's of less importance to keep score who does the most in order to eventually achieve a more durable, more authentic world.

> *To acquire knowledge, one must study;*
> *but to acquire wisdom, one must observe.*
> *(Marylin vos Savant)*

If we face the decline and dangers together, ranking from ... people in power who always want more power at the cost of more lives; from the total decay of moral values around the care for 'life'; from the total lack of subservient integrity; from the corruption of the white collar CEO's and shameless self enrichment; from the powerless, restricted media; from the tainting corruption of everything that wants to stay good, beautiful, unspoiled and unharmed to the polarization between different groups and the risks of upcoming fascism and anarchy ... then we can only resist and fight this with positivism, hope for and faith in a gradual transition to a new system of living and working together under new leadership.

New compass

The crisis advances and infects us like a PC virus, but it is beatable, without falling back to the moralizing ways of the fifties. There still are people who want to be pure and honest when leading large companies and who want to do good for employees and want to help other people in distress.

There will be politicians for whom power and self preservation alone isn't a game anymore, who dare to forget about what the people would want to hear or, especially, what would help their own political party.

When we are willing to accept dependency (and thus: freedom) from the Highest, creating Power again and as we finally understand that we are limited to let others (or anything) grow, we will bow our head or knees, or fold our hands and finally give up Control while realizing our human dependence and limitation. Then we will receive new hope, new perspectives and a new inner compass in return, so that we can rise up again, freed and strengthened, and able to detect, resist and alter corruption, manipulation, misguidance, abuse or controls.

> *Your whishes are a foreboding of that*
> *which you can actually reach. (Goethe)*

'Think before you act' is an old folk wisdom. Thinking is good. Question and examine yourself. Who am I, when no one is watching? What am I, in the overwhelming force of complete silence? How am I, without status, cars, work, holidays, money, insurances, investments and other physical gadgets? What force enables me to give, share and to love?

Unfortunately people judge too quickly and mostly only on the base of what material goods, life style, possessions or positions one collected (or stole, won or received). In the end, after all, it isn't about what you own, but about whom you've become. Evolving towards a better world through trial and error starts ... with you. Today. Now. You have a place somewhere in the social pyramid system, and if that place happens to be at the bottom, know that the whole pyramid will come tumbling down (including the people in power on top) if you walk away from your position.

Apparently, they need you down there! You have power. There is hope. It will be ok. Make the first tiny step for improvement.

Show your soul

> 'We were made for these times. I have heard from so many recently who are deeply and properly bewildered. They are concerned about the state of affairs in our world now. Ours is a time of almost daily astonishment and often-righteous rage over the latest degradations of what matters most to civilized, visionary people. You are right in your assessments. The luster and hubris some have aspired to while endorsing acts so heinous against children, elders, everyday people, the poor, the unguarded, the helpless, is breathtaking. Yet, I urge you, ask you, gentle you, to please not spend your spirit dry by bewailing these difficult times. Especially do not lose hope. Most particularly because, the fact is that we were made for these times. Yes. For years, we have been learning, practicing, been in training for and just waiting to meet on this exact plain of engagement. We are needed, that is all we can know. And though we meet resistance, we more so will meet great souls who will hail us, love us and guide us, and we will know them when they appear. Didn't you say you were a believer? Didn't you say you pledged to listen to a voice greater? Didn't you ask for grace? Don't you remember that to be in grace means to submit to the voice greater?
>
> One of the most calming and powerful actions you can do to intervene in a stormy world is to stand up and show your soul. Soul on deck shines like gold in dark times. The light of the soul throws sparks, can send up flares, builds signal fires, causes proper matters to catch fire.

To display the lantern of soul in shadowy times like these – to be fierce and to show mercy toward others; both are acts of immense bravery and greatest necessity. Struggling souls catch light from other souls who are fully lit and willing to show it. If you would help to calm the tumult, this is one of the strongest things you can do.

There will always be times when you feel discouraged. I too have felt despair many times in my life, but I do not keep a chair for it. I will not entertain it. It is not allowed to eat from my plate. The reason is this: In my uttermost bones I know something, as do you. It is that there can be no despair when you remember why you came to Earth, who you serve, and who sent you here. The good words we say and the good deeds we do are not ours. They are the words and deeds of the One who brought us here. In that spirit, I hope you will write this on your wall: When a great ship is in harbor and moored, it is safe, there can be no doubt. But that is not what great ships are built for'.

Clarissa Pinkola Estes, Ph.D (Author of the best seller Woman who run with wolves)

Every few hundred years in Western history there occurs a sharp transformation. Within a few short decades, society – its worldview, its basic values, its social and political structures, its arts, its key institutions – rearranges itself. And the people born hen cannot even imagine a world in which their grandparents lived and into which their own parents were born. We are currently living through such a transformation. Peter Drucker (1993), Post-Capitalist Society Should we be fearful?

3.

The Fear

The first step on the path to change is acknowledging that not all progress is a blessing and not every new control, monitoring system or regulation will improve your quality of living or society in general.

Wanting to bring about change is basically a choice for more vulnerability and the willingness to think outside the consumptive system of growth, the 'more-more-more', the 'me, I and myself' and the 'want-want-want'. This will only work if you yourself let go of some of the pseudo-securities. Especially top managers and members of the board of directors should be easily capable of this mentally, if only because their employees need it.

Newfound confidence deserves to be fed and directed, and not just regulated and monitored. The world is looking for alternatives for a new 'state of mind'. Now it's your turn. Take charge by adopting a subservient attitude, while inspiring others to increase their levels of hope again. Setting a good example will make others follow that example, although this is true the bad way around as well.

> *Every time we choose safety,*
> *we reinforce fear. (Cheri Huber)*

Being able to implement and show your new spiritual licentiousness and your freedom from fear and your new commitment to the growth of others requires some self-examination. Where lay my inhibitions, my limitations and why do I harbour fear for whom or for what? First off, you have to decide to recognize your fears from now on (together with your hired coach if necessary) and have more faith in a happy ending and the, sometimes intangible external Guidance. Every human conscience was partly fed with some form of original love, once. Appeal to this again and from now on, underpin your choices just a little bit differently, a little bit more authentic.

Free
Your new main authentic drives will be: pleasure, passion and sharing happiness, creating unity and actually applying selflessness usefully. By now you will have learned to trust and you are more gentle, more congenial, nicer and far more patient. There is the fruit of an inner certainty of 'being sure and secure' as well as feeling a 'strong and steady trust' that all will be well, whatever happens. It is a new level of 'knowing' within you. And through your actions, attitude and behaviour this also grows in others.

You have now become one of those authentic and responsible human beings, so much that you even have complete confidence in giving the final decision, whether you go to heaven or hell after you die, out of your hands and your controls into those of your Creator. Then you will be truly free today (and 'led out of Egypt' as it were) and you will not want to lose that confident feel, despite all the emotional peaks and valleys still to come in your lifetime.

*If you are distressed by anything external, the
pain is not due to the thing itself, but to your estimate of it;
and this you have the power to revoke at any moment.
(Marcus Aurelius)*

Now, true happiness isn't dependent on opinions, judgments or the number of possessions of others anymore, and especially not on the rules of status of your (unconscious) reference frame or group. Only then will you see how often fear and manipulation is used in the media, communication, politics, churches and economy. Fear is THE most important reason to make influential decisions on all sorts of areas.

To put it in (valuable) religious terms: fear comes from the devil and love is from God. With human beings, while bound to the laws of nature, as a major 'decision influencer' in the middle, who are in possession of the valuable and potentially powerful 'own responsibility'.

Structures

Do you find the above exaggerated, frightened bla bla? Fact is that one million Dutchmen run, skate, cycle or practice fitness to lower their stress levels and one million Dutchmen eat more than is good for them for exactly the same reason. And then there are half a million Dutchmen (16 million total) taking fear inhibitors or sleeping pills. For a small part of society, the triangle fear, anger and depression is the fertile soil for extremism, wherein they seek their salvation (Henk Kraaijenhof).

Our primal reaction on these emotions is an intuitive choice between running and fighting. Running expresses itself mentally in feelings of helplessness, powerlessness or depression. Fighting translates to feelings of anger, rage or aggression. This affects your employees, colleagues and managers as well.

Problems cannot be solved by the same level of thinking that created them. (Einstein)

In organizations fear translates itself to more restraint and control measures. We make everyone responsible for a small part, so that no one is responsible for the whole or feels any responsibility over the total. This only stimulates everyone working on his or her own 'island' and by no means looks over the fence. The only things thrown over the fence are problems, preferably without clarification or any intention of co-responsibility.

Islands

True integral cooperation is thus made very difficult and a lot of organization consultancies earn a pretty living making processes and procedures in order to entice colleagues to think about each other again. It's a shame though, that often only colleagues or other internal departments are chosen as a starting point for improvements, and not the external customers, clients, members, constituents or the patients, while in the end, they represent what's it all about. Their interests and importance should be the base of the internal motivation and all those working hours.

Constant inspection and verifying became an art during the past 65 years of economic prosperity, through all kinds of (Japanese and American) quality systems (TQM) and organizational strategies (6Sigma). For the mentality of today, it's often counterproductive, needlessly correcting and barren to keep on using control systems from the past. It's often about controlling 'what already is' and not about innovation, creating possibilities and focusing on output for the future anymore. The constant aspiring for bigger organizations entirely fits the old approach. Schools and hospitals became factories and factories became concealed 'finishing venues'. Layer after layer of fresh bureaucracy was introduced and new managers appointed, while the professionals, doing the real work, got snowed in.

Company merges often only serve the interests of 'the top managers' and no longer those of the 'factory floor workers'. Organizations are seen as production units and not as a social interaction and meeting place wherein people should be at the centre. Maximum profit and efficiency are the motivations behind decisions (instead of an optimal atmosphere between employees). But this is about to change. Slowly we are seeing the value of operating on smaller scale again (think of micro credits) and we gradually accept a marginal financial loss, when we become aware of the fact that the real turnover and real valuable profit is in the renewed attention to each other, as well as interested, sympathizing contact and care for the society and care for our surroundings and environment.

> *Too many people are thinking of security*
> *instead of opportunity. They seem to be more*
> *afraid of life than death. (James Bymes)*

There is some sort of physical, natural law to be discovered in this: every attempt to centralize will, at the same time, give birth to a need for decentralization. And: every discovery of a universal greatness is accompanied by a definition of our microscopic smallness. The more we see our universe as all-embracing (because of, for instance, the Hubble space telescope), the more we discover, simultaneously, that even the smallest molecular parts known to man, aren't actually the smallest parts (think of the CERN large hadrons collider, and the 'impact tests'). The sole activity of observation (of events and things) is giving shape to our reality, or so it seems. All that you give attention to, grows.

The future is Now

Fear is experienced in the present, and it originates from the worries for the future. Fear usually has something to do with the mental, physical and material preparation for the possible loss of our life, or the health and wellbeing. The wellbeing of those we love, but also with wellbeing in general, loss of territory, possessions or sources of loss of income. It might also have something to do with the loss of respect, control or the attention and love of others. We live in turbulent and threatening times and so we feel and notice more fearful behaviour. We notice it with ourselves and with others.

The feeling of insecurity increases as does fear. We seem to live in an era that drags itself on from crisis to crisis. By now, we have the environmental crisis, the threat of terrorism, the vaccination crisis, de climate crisis, the financial crisis, the crisis of authority and above all, the crisis of trust. We, society, have meanwhile adopted these fears, and sometimes even succeed in forcing back the fear by taking a simple measure: concentrating on the NOW, while thinking about the life motto: Yesterday is history, tomorrow is a secret and today is a gift.

It all happens NOW, and in 'the moment of NOW' we find our concentration and our highest productivity. This might be quite hard for leaders, ministers and executives, because people expect ideas about the future and how to cope with it from them. Besides, I don't hear a single CEO these days talking about long term scenario's for his company or about plans going forward for, let's say, ten years. At most only plans for the medium term, up to about five years, seem to have some sense of reality.

> *The best thing about the future is that it only comes one day at a time. (Abraham Lincoln)*

Expulsion

This loss of insight in the future can be traced back to the media (ruled by fads), politics (governing is no longer looking ahead but only a matter of desiring to score this day), the top of big corporations (options, bonuses, a culture of settling scores, walking away from responsibility and making quick bucks in the short term) and to the employees (assertive and even aggressive, demanding behaviour and brutality in attitude, thinking and doing). Fortune still favours the bold and the brutes.

If we don't have that in us, that primal brutality, we run away out of fear and stress towards all kinds of precautionary measures, apathy, indifference, loss of pleasure and less effective and sparkling functioning, in our personal life as well as in organizations. That, or we join a protesting movement or group, like for instance the Tea Party in America. Our anger and aggressions can also be expressed in the form of antisocial behaviour, passive aggression, vandalism and hooliganism or in the form of shootings at schools, universities or rebellion within companies. Just watch the news.

Sometimes this destructiveness turns inwards, in the form of suicide. A recent example can be found at France Telecom, where in 2009 quite a substantive number of employees took their own lives, because they couldn't handle the fear and insecurity of one redundancy round after another. For redundancy does not only have financial consequences, but social consequences (loss of structure, purpose in life and the group to which one belonged) as well.

Expulsion and removal are very influential measures and a huge punishment for the social mammal: the human being. It isn't for nothing that, when we were young, we were to stand in the hallway at school, or sent from the dinner table as a punishment. Sometimes we came around, but more often we found a way to take vengeance, some way or the other. Behold, this is a biological base for micro misery, loneliness, feelings of abandonment and detachment.

Dreaming out loud

The coming ten years it is again time for another 'shift & change', only now with a move towards new humanitarian involvement and renewed appreciation for authenticity and the human scale of things. A move towards responsible, subservient and connecting executives, who want to set an unselfish example. Towards durability in the (re)cycling of raw materials, the realization of how much we really waste and the too great a differences in the distribution of wealth.

Slowly personal greed is disappearing and is translated to the public wellbeing of all. Governments are again here to serve their citizens. We are noticing more subservient market forces originating from a new culture- a new, different state of mind – of mutual trust and a shared responsibility for a good, rational balance between self interest, the interest of others, society and the planet. The yield will then go to those who provide palpable products and tangible services, who labour for money every day and not just to those who speculate (even with the savings of citizens), gamble on the stock market or fractionally finance without any underlying counter value other than a future IOU promise. David C. Korten notices a couple of shifts and values in his Mindful Markets, which are happening right now:

Capitalism	**Mindful Markets**
Principle:	
Money	*Life*
Dominant:	
More money for the few	*Use money to provide needs of all*
Company size:	
Preferably bigger & bigger	*Small and medium*

Investments:
For maximum profit *Increase the useful output for all*
Competition:
Eliminate them ... *Stimulating innovation and efficiency*
Cooperation:
To escape competition *Helping the common good forward*
Trade:
Free *Honest*

As a reasonable guaranty against the self enrichment, egoism and greed of the few, Kortens' idea is an appealing perspective, to combine with the valuable range of ideas of among others David Schweickart in order to create a system of economical democracy, where the efficiency of the market is combined with the democracy in the decision making processes.

Transition

In the economical democracy, all people working there make decisions democratically, in a cooperative model. This means they aren't made by the private owner, the multinational or the shareholders and other owners of raw materials or available production methods. The new economical design and the new scale of trade and markets are smaller, local and trade (finally) takes place by personal contact again. Management decisions are taken according to the 'one man; one vote or voice' system instead of the more familiar 'one euro; one vote' principle, which is presently so dominant.

If a leader is wanted, or if leadership is needed, he will be chosen by the employees or by the citizens and not parachuted in or instituted by a few rulers from outside the organization.
Problem is that a theoretical model, no matter how good or bad it is, is nothing more than an (excellent) framework for theoretical

thinking. What it's really about is the transition period from one system to the other; from the one cycle to the next. Preferably, this will progress gradually, but for gradualness we need selfless moral leaders for the coming years, who will serviceably bring the visions into practice after which we, as humanity, crave for and which we need so much at this challenging time in history.

So, would the next M. Ghandi or N. Mandela please stand up?
One downside is, however, that the ruling sitting powers (in front of, and behind the screens and by now globally organized and intertwined) will not let go of control, merely based on regional or local resistance, like already happened once in India or South Africa.

But fear not, as a manager, director or owner you NOW have the possibility of already making some small steps in the right direction, namely of cooperating in a more humanitarian way. If need be, still as a small section within the old regime of naked and hard ego capitalism where we still find ourselves in. Employees really want to experience this new involvement from your side and will want to contribute. They really want to build and cooperate and give their time and energy again based on mutual trust, especially for credible vision and missions, so they can help realizing these with newfound commitment, by providing meaningful, honest services and by providing helpful, 'real' products.

Offer from authenticity

Employees have grown and have become more independent since the economical golden Age, which spanned from WWII to about the Y2K moment. The dependence of the organizational working relationships at a single location has rapidly decreased. The phenomenon of having to hold up appearances, your so-called status and tittle-tattle for the neighbours, is disappearing, as information is available everywhere and worldwide.

Substantial expertise is now available at the bottom of the organizations as well, and can be consulted in 'real time' and studied online. Transparency has become, out of inner drive and necessity, the magic word. Integrity and SQ (spiritual intelligence) form the base for new management theories and The Truth is finally a part of the new content and messages in advertising & PR. We aren't there yet, but we're getting close.

Turning shop -under pressure of any conflict of interest or not- backroom politics, tyrannical behaviour, 'old boys' networks, the ability to exercise power based on position or bloodline ... in a while it will only turn against those who are still fully enjoying the benefits now. Target groups have ceased to exist, and wanting to target these anyway is old marketing language. The course to be followed is formulated in co-creation and 'bottom-up' (not 'top-down' anymore) and quotes like 'conquering the market' have become management language from the past.
Consumers now participate online, they 'buzz' and share their opinions of approval or disapproval on the many forums. Agitating, abusing and communicating via new media such as Twitter, or commenting on online news-and newspaper sites.
There seems to be space for everyone's inalienable, unique 'Point of View' and there also seems to be a need for everyone's individual expression, and no longer to just those of highly educated managers, opinion leaders and academics.

As soon as we all can show, argue and prove, through these new media and many social networks, that dealing with capital goods and the environment responsibly is more productive and socially acceptable, companies will be quicker to accept and even embrace this. Out of free will (or peer pressure) and from subservient motives in order to make it better for everyone in this world.

With respect to that, it already is a major step forward if the few first supermarkets up and to a few car manufacturers are willing to produce and sell more 'durably and greener' goods. If need be, helped by stimulating regulations and governmental sanctions. This pressure is a typical example as a helpful phenomenon that is necessary during an evolutionary transition situation.

The answer

The biggest changes that come about are however preferably based on a feeling of urgency and motivation from our hearts. Inner conviction and passion are the constructive, binding and constant factors for future economic success (no matter how it is financed). Offering products or services will then be regarded as credible, for there is a real passion behind it, coming from the DNA of the organization and from the unique conscience of its leaders. Only this will bring about something that will strike root in the longer term. Sanctions and outside pressure are good, but free will and inner urgency are better. That goes for every politician up and to every chairman of a board of directors.

> *Showing bravery and compassion is an act of integrity and of the highest significance. (Clarissa Estes)*

Summarized: it is high time to become authentic and to move from pseudo-security to inner security. Let the old stimulus – reward mechanisms go and start to really talk to people again and meet them. Learn to connect again and say farewell to all the old administrational and managerial masks. Dare to let people grow by new management principles of sharing and giving. An authentic inner drive or 'state of mind' goes just a bit further and deeper than, for instance, the old marketing method of showing a big cheque with the company logo on a podium at a 'help us solve all the misery TV benefit', just for the free airtime.

That is still charity of which you yourself benefit the most. What you do out of authentic values, you do from conviction, and not because it makes you look good. That deception will always come to light and does not benefit the credibility and the trust in your organization. People want genuineness and look for integrity and concern and want to see passion and authenticity. No more mannerism. As reward, mistakes and shortcomings will be forgiven all the quicker. It must feel strange, when noticing this for the first time. Just like the first time you really needed help with something in your normal life, dared to ask for it and actually got it! Just like that! With no strings attached. Selfless. If you have never experienced or endured that, you are way behind in the new authentic society.

New objectivity

Share your future vision from your own conviction and listen to your heart more. Open your blinded eyes and 'reset' your needs and help others doing that the same. Investigate your acquired management and economical automatism again and already decide to become at least 10% more of an idealist and a rebel. At the same time, decide to become 100% authentic ... in the long run. Decide this for your organization as well. And you'll probably have guessed by now: result follows intention. So embrace the intention for authenticity, do something with it and expect results from this.

Not all improvement and change can be chased at the same time, nor can it produce a fully developed plan or result the next day. There is a time for everything. Do not, for instance, start an ad hoc CAC (Corporate Authenticity Committee) which has to produce a report within the coming month, 'or else'... for that is the old way of managing. Of course some form of deadlines, matter of factness and stress will never cease to exist, but no longer let that be a target in itself (just to have a target), like the weird idea to change, just for change sake.

Next to that there will of course always be clear, business contracts, also in the next economic distribution (as a testimony of mutual trust) and if one gives something (of himself) he may expect something equal in return. If need be by explicitly asking or pointing for or to something. Mutuality is a beautiful and logical thing, and so is clarity. Unspoken expectations will be extremely hard to manage in the future as well. Also, we will all stay responsible for our own, appropriate output. The new economic democracy is by no way a commune.

Credibility

Trust and credibility at all sorts of levels have been seriously damaged over the last few years. The peak has been the way politics have been practiced in The Netherland, with a dramatic lack of visible leadership, substantial expertise and without backbone, especially during the drama in the financial sector and the following social crisis. Citizens now pay the price and save, through taxes, the already rich finance sector and bankers.

The people are hit hard in their core existence and nature: through naïve faith in authority (because of the national Dutch characteristic 1: acting as a finger pointing vicar) and through the savings account (because of the national Dutch characteristic 2: being the money making merchant). Citizens in many countries have been used and abused and the first national traumas become visible through the outlet of populism, extremism, intolerance, fascism, police state law making and the need for a strong leader. This is an accident waiting to happen. From Greece and France to Spain and Holland to the USA.

The main questions for leaders and citizens will be: what information can I trust? From whom? How can I be of help to a new, honest and equal mutuality? What do I want, what can I do, what may I give to help others become more authentic? What does it mean for me as a CEO that I look after 'an organization'? For new answer you might just look upwards more (=pray more), and you'll definitely look more to your inside voice and authentic consciousness.

> *Daring to recognize dependence*
> *Is the beginning of autonomy. (Pleu)*

If you dare to know and show who you are, be available more, embrace loyalty and stop the camouflaging 'busy-busy-busy' behaviour, you'll create new chances for everyone. Organizations and managers will finally give increased meaning and substance to their existence and their environments. What do I mean for the other, the environment and the society? Your valued contribution to the offline world and to the new virtual online networks depends on basic self-knowledge and the life choices you've made. Your new strategy and approach to join the huge variety of possibilities through the new social networks, does not require hiding yourself behind faked marketing masks or tactical manoeuvres in order to stay ahead of the competition.

The only chance of succeeding online and offline lies in the ability of being able to know, share and present yourself, your strength and your authenticity. Who are you as a person and as an organization? What can you do (or your company do) that no one else can? How do you (or your company) contribute to a better, more durable world? Who does your company share with and with whom do you connect? How do you see your contribution? How can it be recognized? How do you remain authentic together as board or management team?

Those are the new questions that, from now on, will demand upright communication and PR and authentic answers and behaviour will become the new 'profitability'. Through acceptance, feedback, appreciation and, eventually, in enough profit through money (although the function of money is again a medium of exchange, like it was once intended (and not as an idol or addiction).

Enough is sufficient

The new authentic life motto is: enough is, by now, more than sufficient. Consequently, enough to share is the new adage ... and the most successful factor for success ... plus the goal to pursue ... and the secret password. When do you have enough? When confidence in the future enables you to suddenly see that you have money and time left today! When you finally notice those items, which really feed your soul and happiness: satisfaction, trust and recognition of your dependence.

Then you will release energy that enables you to see the good, decide what is good and do it. It is that simple (and as a company: yes, it is no problem to start doing 'good' after rebate of costs and the necessary financial reservations for future continuity). Profit maximizing and process optimizing are outdated terms from a time (1950-1999) that everything was possible and nothing seemed impossible. The problem is, not everything is possible anymore. The failure in the human and relational areas and the dichotomy has just become too big anno 2010.

Making corporate authenticity recognizable and transparent provides the dearly needed credibility and internal peace of mind for employees and management. Performances become more consistent and recognizable in time. For now: know your restrictions, already take a step back in the ongoing daily 'rat race', look with your new authentic eyes and you will have a better chance of succeeding in making the best of new, valuable opportunities and in making new authentic relations.

As a result, finally the focus will lie entirely with content and what people really think of certain things or matters and about their visions for everyone. They have value, because also external relations listen to a leader or company that does not just exist for itself, nor only operates for itself. When people invite and value others to help determine the course or make decisions together, it no longer is 'the economic jungle', in which everyone learned to fight, but a sympathizing economy in which decisions and choices can count on an involvement and a true basis originating from that involvement. When passion and conviction serve no one but yourself, your political party, your department or your own wallet, the independent consumer will simply walk away. Or the buying public will get even with you, your company or your political party, quickly, directly and silently ... online. People know what to look for on the web and will find feedback in an instant. They can mobilise resistance or support in hours, also by SMS or Twitter. Individual blogs are the new news channels. Social media are the new opinion leaders. Beware: there is no strategy or place to hide (your motives) anymore! Better be transparent and honest and ... authentic. That is how your company or party will survive.

Passion wins

Within this chain of production and marketing, the planning, targeting, pre checking and controlling of turnover in advance becomes less feasible than it used to be. This is mainly because of the upswing of the internet, the heterogeneous composition of the target groups (or followers or buyers) and the independence with which people can collect knowledge, exchange ideas and value or judge the service or organization publically. Add the growing distrust against the pure motives of executives or politicians and the necessity to communicate and trade in another manner with relations or citizens differently is unavoidable.

The new approach means that it is necessary to let the planning of the sales process; the result and the outcome go a little bit and let go of the control a little as well. Give it some space. Accept some degree of uncertainty. Calculate conventionally. Give it some time. Find out what moves people (the 'software' in a way) and connect with them. Don't always start with measures or procedures that will mainly improve the 'hardware', the systems and processes. Share your expectations as leader and impart the common goals. Focus less on the assignment figures, market shares or turnover successes. Can you feel the difference?

Scout the values and framework around the business or trade and discuss the pros and cons of the product or services or market positions, together with external stakeholders or employees. By just forcing policies and pushing measurement from a distance, vague unknown corporate HQ somewhere you'll create nothing but counter-pressure and demotivation. Take time for someone involved somewhere in the company and his or her world of thinking and experience (which doesn't mean you have to become a social worker or a personal coach for someone, so don't be afraid you have to suddenly perform as nice or likable).

What feels like a tiny intuitive difference to you, might be often already a world of difference for someone else. Besides, it's not like grass will grow faster by pulling it. Taking a bit more time for meetings and showing a bit more interest in people, often inspires a lot more mutual trust. And trust is crucial. Give people in organizations their passions and, if need be, their professions back and regard processes and systems mainly as a supporting necessity.

And so 'another state of mind' comes into being trough a humanitarian attitude and a new, open personal style, with which you operate as a leader. For the wellbeing and the success of others. And like that, also for yourself (and for a relevant quantitative profit and return).

Responsibility
Employees want to carry responsibility if they can connect their contribution and commitment to the common cause and if they get the space needed to practice their expertise. There is a certain level of trust required and the chance to be able and allowed to carry responsibility. How often don't we hear 'what's the point', for 'the boss doesn't listen anyway' and that he has no idea of what's 'really' going on in the lower layers of an organization? Quite often indeed! And that's first and foremost a problem of the management. The reason they are at the top of the organizational pyramid (with a better paycheck than others) is to solve things like these.
Through trust, mankind becomes more than just a factor of production and a humanitarian approach will be pulsating at the heart of the organization. Vision and mission statements will then yield valuable reactions and will no longer be composed pro forma, that is to say empty and hollow. It is no longer just about realizing 'lower, basic' sale targets, but also about contributing to 'higher' values and future dreams. Facilitating that development is no easy task, for employees will only function averagely when systems and 'shared values' do not fit with what is expected or asked of them. External relations will not feel involved if there is no substantive contribution possible, or if they cannot express their opinions, which are not considered of any influence either. This asks for careful balancing between trust and control/management. But please remember that stimulating trust by controlling less is the new 'state of mind' for authentic managers.

If there is to be a human future, we must bring ourselves into balanced relationship with one another and the Earth. This requires building economies with heart. (David Korten)

This will not happen without resistance, of course not, but even this resistance must be handled with more transparency and openness, within smaller or bigger organizations, with low or highly educated people, with elders and youngsters, in bad and good economical times, in multi or monoculture companies, with more, or already a bit less encouragement and control, with the CEO as well as with the colleagues nearby and from an equivalent starting point, in older and newer organizations and ... with a realistic view of subversion and counter productivity during the transformation. No omelette without breaking some eggs. Acting authentically does not automatically mean acting naively or hen-hearted. There are more than enough reasons imaginable to never want to start this process. But, we no longer agree to those reasons, so let's just start!

Since we do not live on the planet Utopia and human greed, lust for power and urge to control will be around for some time to come, we will have to do this step by step. Make a start, talk about it, revise your unique 'point of view' again, if you dare, and ask a question without actually wanting to issue an order. Experience the increasing growth in ideas and creativity and committed behaviour to improve things of the people around you. What's there to lose? Will someone hit you? Will someone now shoot down your colleagues? Will you be out of a job tomorrow? Will your savings be stolen? Do people suddenly regard you as a softie or swab? Do you think you will never be taken seriously again?

Wake up and get real!

4.

The Hope

If we first dwelled on fear as a destructive primal force, then we must also talk about hope as a constructive power supply of energy. Hope is by far the best cure for fear.

This also holds true for managers and politicians with their strategies, policies, motives, attitude and charisma. It is, no doubt, tempting to abandon hope at this point in history and make misuse of the growing fear (see previous chapters). Fatalism and cynicism stand in wait for the people and the employees when the prospect of and the courage for 'something better or different' slowly fades.

Because of the low 'level of hope' in our thinking, desiring and acting, we do ourselves injustice. We retreat as individuals behind the safe mental walls, and close the gates of our heart, dig a trench around our involvement and selflessness and incline like nations to isolationism or localism. Authentic leaders do not do things like these, because it can damage their interest, turnover and businesses and will demotivate their surroundings. A hopeful future brings about energy and the will to build prosperity even further and improve skills and ethics constantly.

Without hope, working has no other use than being present for the money or to receive a paycheck (for the duration of it). Without hope, there won't be many new ideas, for there is no inspiration and participation has no real benefit. Return on mental investment is low. In general, for many people life (and especially for Christians) has no meaning at all, without hope.

Positive

Directors, managers, entrepreneurs, politicians and owners are the ones of whom we all expect that they have, communicate and generate the energy necessary to inspire employees, followers and citizens to contribute to their sensible goals. In order to do that, they look first to their respective futures, extract their vision or faith from it and build a framework around it, so that it translates into a manageable and intelligible step-by-step mission for all. Personally these foremen and forewomen always remain positive and full of energy (and preferably realistic as well), if need be against better judgment. They understand that in every threat along the way, there is that one unique chance as well.

> *Sometimes something has got to happen first*
> *before something happens. (Johan Cruijff)*

Hope inspires people and enables them to accomplish great, sometimes impossible things. Hope is a powerful emotional instrument and to be full of hope is a valuable individual state of mind. Faith in something can be transferred to a certain level, a conviction can still be shared, but hope is something strictly personal. Take a moment to reflect of what it is that you have hoped for yesterday, today, in a moment and later on … it's quite a lot, isn't it! It's no surprise that one much heard statement is: 'I really hope that …' etc.

Faith

Faith is the certainty of the things one hopes for, and the proof of things that cannot be seen (Hebrews 1, NT). Proof means showing something that is true. So faith shows you that things you cannot see are true. The 'things' are there, even though you can't see them (yet). Faith, at the same time proves things that you cannot see yet, are going to exist. Faith thus lets us realize that if something cannot be seen yet, that does not necessarily mean that it is non-existent, or will not be there. Faith verifies the (or: a) hope.

Problem is that not everyone believes the same codes, guidelines or principles and some may even believe in wrong goals or evil people or only -or perhaps completely not- in themselves.

Faith and hope have a lot in common with each other. Somewhere else in The Holy Book is written: 'speak of the hope that is in you now, in a friendly way, and always be prepared to be held responsible for it'. Now that is what I call a clear handle to hold on to for a modern manager or politician, who is communicating a vision. 'Yes we can' and 'Just do it' weren't such hugely successful campaign and company slogans for nothing. What an effect will it have then, when inspiring people for new hope will no longer be about your own ego first or your own interests or those of the peer group or political party first, but more about the wellbeing of all employees, citizens, the surroundings and the life in nature.

> *Where there is no vision, there is no hope.*
> *(George Washington Carver)*

Hope is the uncertain expectation that a certain event you desire will take place. Despair occurs when the chance of that happening seems gone, when fear strikes or when this (uncertain) expectation produces an unwanted event.

False hope means that that expectation is entirely fantasy. Wikipedia also states hope can be passive – like a wish – but active as well. Hope can also really shape things, meaning that there is work to be done and that effort is required. Simply wishing for them does not bring any of your goals closer. Hope is situated in between knowing and wishing, but is no 'wishful thinking'. Hope certainly has something to do with trust as well. And my one wish is, eh… no: my hope is that there will be more trust between people, business relations and trade.

Hope scientific

Duthman Roland van der Vorst distinguishes four different kinds of hope: Christian hope, hope of performance, mental hopes and hope of opportunity. There are four sources of which hope can come from:

1. A desire for a better world
2. The expectation that everything will someday be all right (because of outside intervention)
3. Our own possibilities and performances, or the power to break through a rut in order to get a good feeling
4. The hope of opportunity, which is pragmatic and will get substance or meaning at an appropriate time to come. Hope is more than an emotion. It is a neurological chemical brain condition as a reaction to our existence at this moment, a 'state of being', which changes our perspective and so our future way of acting. Never underestimate the power of people full of hope.

That hope costs a lot of money, and is worth spending a lot of money on, is as logical as it is clear. For instance, we like to hope for (or simply buy) golden mountains, status, redemption, recognition, happiness or forgiveness. Whether it actually produces a lot or little (the jackpot or the consolation prize in the lottery) … hope even determines what we buy. If need be, for a whole lifetime, every month we spend a predetermined amount for the hope to get rich, considered attainable through the monthly ad random draw of lottery numbers.

Hell

I once heard a picturesque statement from a protestant foreman about the true nature of hell. The image of an ever-burning pool of fire is still present here and there, but the idea of forever being a part of people who have even lost the smallest sparkle of hope is frankly horrifying. A human being or human behaviour without (a source or sparkle of) hope is … terrifying.

Hope makes life enjoyable, and faith does pass it (hope) on, conviction asks for pursuing hope and with love added as well, you will never tremble for anything or anyone again.

> *The torture of a bad conscience is*
> *the hell of a living soul. (John Calvin)*

C.R. (Rick) Snyder has developed a theory about just this. Leaders with a higher percentage of hope are clearer about their expectations or goals, see ways to reach those and are active in the pursuing their goals and conquering resistances and blockades. Or: where there is a will, there is a way. Good, hope inspiring people are partly dreamers, but are also able to move people. This combination characterizes an authentic leader.

Spreading hope makes us unique individuals. With hope we are a source of energy and strength for others that successfully work (or fight or wrestle or struggle) together, from a phase of dreams towards the desired result. The measure in which we hope has influence on the measure in which we are and will be able to realize the desired outcome. Not just a desired future but preferable a better future as well, as seen from the actual situation.

In dark economic times, you hope for better times together with your subjects, followers, employees or neighbours and with creativity you find solutions in order to take them with you. When you speak out loud of a new event or hoped outcome for at least four times, and keep repeating it, you'll eventually start believing it yourself. Guaranteed! Don't forget to look back at it, with both feet on the ground, as the outcome doesn't seem to become reality or is attainable anymore.

What hope does

A higher level of hope does not only help you realize your goals, but also simply gives you a much better feeling. According to Barbera Fredrickson, cherishing hope is an expression of functioning optimally, which enriches our way of thinking, makes us more creative and less vulnerable for the (uncertain) future as well. Hope can be called upon and shows itself right at the moment we are afraid, depressed or endure a setback. With the help of hope we will come out on top much quicker. Please, let this mean something for the performance or the statements of our leaders in times of economic depression or reorganization.

> *When things are bad, we take comfort in the thought that they could always be worse. And when they are, we find hope in the thought that things are so bad they have to get better. (Unknown)*

For a lot of positive people, tapping into feelings of hope and ideas isn't all that hard. Take a minute and wonder about the amount of hope available. It is quite a lot and quite a number of subject and statements will automatically come to mind. You are a blessed human being, blessed with perspective and you feel like living and realizing your 'hope-target' and making your 'hope-wish' come true.

Leaders without hope do not inspire. They see no way out of the problems and do not want to initiate new events. In all negative events, something positive can also be found. There really is. Went bankrupt? You probably learned what real business is all about! No more money? It makes you more creative! Out of a job? Also write a, so it turned out later on, invaluable diary for your children! Threatened by rumours of war? Finally you are realizing what it's all about. Ill? Take the chance of doing what is still possible and leave the unimportant matters for later!

Through hope we continue to learn and improve, even if it doesn't directly benefit ourselves. The end is always a new beginning. Just a bit different from what you though it was or was told perhaps and maybe accompanied with severe physical suffering or mental pain. Sure, the misery in this world is so extensive that we cannot possibly comprehend it or solve it. Yes, it's a sad thing to see. Even within your organization, humanity is 'broken', imperfect and perhaps guilty before the eyes of God. Just like you. Remain hopeful, share the faith and start with small improvements directly around you. When we see the deepest misery, we also see where we could do better. Do not lose hope upon statement alone. Just DO good.

The 'Hope Theory'
When you take pause by the possibilities of hope more often, you will automatically hope for more and for a more hopeful outcome and hope generating results. What a strange, confirmatory phenomena! Practice improves skills and inspires positivism and happiness. The 'hope theory' assumes that the measure of difficulty and effort required to actually reaching a future result or hoped for

goal, is determinative for the level of joy or satisfaction from attaining it (C.R. Snyder). That is some beckoning and realistic perspective!

So the goal to spend the evening watching TV (= easy) will be less satisfactory than training for a marathon if you've been an office mouse for the last 55 years (= a bit harder, but attainable). Thus the hope theory discourages people as well. Especially when we hope for unreasonable and improbable things. Think of the hope for 'peace on earth'. There is no way this will summon masses of energy; it's a truly impossible goal (with just human efforts).

This also means that it is crucial for politicians and managers to maintain realistic about visions and missions. But challenging enough to address higher levels of new energy ('within 5 years we walk on the moon' of JF Kennedy was a good one'). You have no idea how much dedication you will mobilize – after the initial scepticism of course- by pursuing a meaningful goal and an authentic target. Think of the Dutch entrepreneur Victor Muller when he stood before the Saab employees in Sweden (2010) and think of the brand Rekkof (the word Fokker turned around), which got loaned millions by the Financial Department for a next flying Dutch dream ... it is top level dosed 'possibility thinking'.

Keep the risk well in mind though. It is not entirely open-ended when you arouse the 'hope energy' of employees of citizens. Think of the downfall of ABNAMRO bank and CEO Rijkman Groenink who eventually gave in to the Parliamentary committee De Wit (2009): 'the goal to try and win a place in the top 5 was a rookie mistake and, in hindsight, set the tone for the downfall' (loosely translated).

Mistakes

Dutch prime minster JP Balkenende (2002-2010) once promised the Dutch: 'After the economic sour, the sweet will come'. But the sweet never came. Much worse though, was that he never fell back on it, went further into it and did not dared to reflect, accept responsibility or admit that is was not attainable.

Consequence: for years to come the statement will be quoted and scoffed and a large piece of his credibility has disappeared. So this statement did not inspire any extra personal and national trust (as one of the two areas of return for being Corporate Authentic: credibility and trust). Besides, it is sheer impossible for JPB to repeat or generate high hopes again. On top, for that to happen we should also shake off our big Dutch national characteristic: pretending nothing happened and just move on.

But if the choice of vision is right and fitting, the realization already begins at verbalizing and visualizing it (entirely according to 'The Secret'). The closed curtains of fear and desperation can open and suddenly we all see the bigger picture and direction. A multitude of creativity and energy will be released. In short, the more we hope, the less we fear. And that delivers a considerably better feeling. In healthcare, for instance, hope proves to be helpful during recovery.

Hope does sometimes make one live, literally. Hope is an incentive. To hope is to do. Hope for a better future made voters in the USA vote en masse for a presidential candidate Obama (2009). 'Hope is a strategy', he once said ... and that's where it all went entirely wrong! Hope doesn't allow itself to be utilized in such an impersonal rational strategically tactical way. It is inextricably connected to the person and his or her authenticity. Obama may count himself lucky if he survives on this strategic thinking. In other words: do not arouse any hope if you haven't intrinsically gone through it yourself (and that you can, for you are an authentic leader, foreman or chef).

Action

Hope is the uncertain expectation of a future event, where 'faith' is the certain element. There are two other sides of hope: despair (when the chance of the desired event seems lost) or fear (when the expectation threatens to have or has an unwanted effect). False hope means the expectation is based entirely on fantasy or you hope for an event with a particularly small chance of realization. Faith in that must really become stronger and stronger in order to be able to continue.

Furthermore, hope can also be passive, turned inward as a wishful thought, but prefers to be active. Without that element of action, hoping for something would be fairly simple and probably not about a real desired, future change (Wikipedia).

> *When we stop blaming others, we especially discover our amazing self. (Pleu)*

Change demands action. If you only hope without taking any action from your side, all you can do is blame others (of the status quo, for instance) and remain being a victim. An organizational vision with hope, but without any concrete translation of that hope, thus achieves nothing and will gain nothing but a negative boomerang effect, because of those who feel cheated and conned by it. Think of the politicians who preach nothing but 'hope' (Obama, Wilders in his campaign) and never present concrete policies or solutions. Hope is not a strategy or goal, only plans of action move people.

A plan of approach and suitable actions increase the certainty the hoped for success. Taking the right direction together, following the just cause relies on how the hope, plan or vision is communicated and shared in combination with feedback, amendments or adjustments. After that the acceptance will grow and the measure of faith in the relevance of one's own contribution to the vision.

A widely heard statement is this framework: 'an idea is good, a plan is better'. Or: 'there is no lack of new ideas, only of people able to realize them'.

False Hope

So just formulate the actions and execute the plan. And if it's not working, or parts of it aren't, adjust it according to the participation and contribution of involved relations (through crowd sourcing or open sourcing). Not by psychological trickery please. The marketing approach of Revlon cosmetics was once a well-known one. They didn't sell lipstick, but hope (that it made women more beautiful and more attractive). Does this still hold true? Buy my service or product, realize your dreams and become happy?

Yes, or at least partly. We still let people sell us the hope, no matter how grown-up and highly educated we are, that we are unique, irreplaceable and that we can be more beautiful and smarter by using brand x or y. Especially when it comes to bodily decay, health, kids and cars. This approach is however getting a bit passé for the sane, authentic man. It is considered old marketing now we have all become well informed, independently thinking employees, citizens and consumers. Right? I fear not. Not yet. In order to do so, we must first learn to see through manipulation techniques better (see the chapter authentic communication).

Giving hope should be something else than creating dependence at the same time. Desiring something to improve is ok, but no one trusts a politician who soothes us and wishes us to 'go quietly to sleep', for 'everything will be all right' anymore these days. That would currently be considered as a first class contra-indicator. So: wake up and take your own responsibility. Look for information yourself and become able to compare information yourself and ask questions, share your opinion. This has become a lot simpler than it used to be, thanks to the internet.

There is no true faith possible without deeds
to bring the believed desire nearer. (Pleu)

Stimulus

Authentic leaders offer an insight, further along the way of life, to which you'll come to desire. Also important: they make sure that it can be attained together with an extra effort and the necessary sacrifices. Through their clear visions and clearly formulated missions, they stimulate (their) people to persevere. So make sure, as a leader of this era that your employees or constituents will receive hope (again). According to Irvin Yalom, figurehead of the existential psychotherapy, that may be the most important factor in the practice of psychotherapeutic therapy. Hope is related to better work performances, successes and general wellbeing.

The nice part is that there is hope for everyone in your organization, from high to low and not just for a select group. You want change fast? Communicate your hope for fast change, and it will already start to work. Take note: you are working with 'human capital' and that is never without liability.

Your motives, passion and drive are decisive for the appeal of your ideas and your ability to convince. It's just what you're hoping for, isn't it? Or might it be better and more assertive to speak of: … what you're counting on?

In Holland we used to express the hope that you'd informed people well enough at the bottom of our letters of application and about the hopeful expectation of a personal follow-up conversation. A few decades ago, that was considered too 'soft' and there ought to have stood something more assertive, that you were 'counting' on a follow-up. That time, of bluff and masked overestimation of oneself, does not fit in the 'state of another mind' authentic man. Hope is the new keyword and already 'counting on' something in advance is yesterday's approach. The level of uncertainty that is accompanied by the expression of hope, just provides that little bit of extra space required for an own valuable interpretation or an additional contribution of someone else. This way, ee enrich each other.

> *Hope sees the invisible, feels the intangible*
> *and achieves the impossible. (Unknown)*

Again, we are forced to think about what's really important in this time of crisis, with concern to the use of capital goods, raw materials, time and money, nature, our attitude and our state of mind towards others, our motives and what interests and binds us. Determining the source from which we are able to believe or pursue is next, if it concerns business (in personal life it is usually the other way around). If we operate the other way around in our working environment as well, we'll easily get trapped in a religious dispute, characterized by 'true and not true and 'them and we'.

By the way, that religion has a very important place as the origin of hope has been clear for some centuries. Alan Mittleman claims that even secular thinkers (like Ernst Block, Immanuel Kant and Hannah Arendt) cannot give a real explanation why hope takes up such an important central place in our life, without having to confess there is indeed something sacred. Hope inspires faith, just as faith inspires hope. Hope asks for faith and faith calls for action.

Yes we can

Too often, we focus on our own problems, frustrations and suffering. Searching for feelings of hope and intentionally formulating thoughts f hope are not possible. A lot of people can't even get rid of problems without help or professional attention. The prospect of improvement and hope is their first need and foremost desire, together with less pain, an end to disquietedness, felt shortage or reduced abuse. Listening as prime skill for understanding and helping is therefore an art, and wanting to listen actively and probing even further, even more so. When you're all busy on your own schedule as manager, full of yourself, truly helping someone and subservient contact becomes impossible.

Authentic people learn to be less frightened of that real contact, the real emotion and the real pains, which are part of showing compassion through a hopeful, therefore positive attitude.
'Faith is as big as a seed of mustard can and will move mountains', or so the biblical statement goes. Behind this lies the hope, as some kind of subconscious trust that everything is possible after all. If you just believe and have faith, despite whatever the harsh reality shows us or wants you to believe. Hope is pure energy and can bring up, bring about and mean quite a lot.

> *Blessed are they, who do not see and still believe.*
> *(Johannes 20:29 NT)*

We often constantly balance between hope and fear, faith and disbelief and hope pulls and drags us more and more to the positive side, sometimes against better judgment. Someone who speaks about hope draws all attention and interest, and we become curious about the source and the reason behind it. What can we achieve together with hope? How can it become better for all, even a little bit? What and who declares war to our negative thoughts and egocentric feelings? Where is the all-embracing story and the urgency to really want to change? Who will touch me in my heart and soul? What treasure really lies at the end of the rainbow? What story is great enough to hope and live for? With who may or must I live or work with to achieve true happiness? How will I arrive at my destination? Seek, and thou shall find; knock, and the door shall be opened to you (loosely translated from the New Testament).

5.

The Yield Factor: Trust

Trust and credibility are the two keywords by which managers can observe and measure whether the new authentic way of thinking is generating any results.

Acceptation, appreciation, dignity, friendship, compassion, connection and safety are the sweet fruits of authenticity. It's these fruits that count, as a reward when you 'let go' more, be more 'vulnerable' and accepting some guidance from outside, whether that is via another person, destiny or ... God. Too bad though, that abuse and misuse of already given trust are instantly on the prowl again.

That is some risk of giving your trust away and wanting to receive it yourself. We have to accept that systematic decay of 'what is good and selfless' will never disappear completely in others (and in the deepest, darkest reaches of our own souls). But let's not get discouraged. Only if the intentions and motivations behind our actions are sincere and in the interest of others, is trust coming from authenticity truly a positive contribution and constructive experience. People simply buy more products over a longer period of time from companies, which can be trusted. Translation: make trustworthy products and supply idem services, actively holding on to original values. Like the ones the company was once founded on. And allow external judgement to sharpen up the original (once good) intentions.

Trust is the currency of the new world. (Steven Covey)

Growth of trust begins with your own individual decision to start and 'trust more'. And you will become more subservient for all, when you have learned to trust yourself a little better. 'Love another like you can love yourself' is a wise insight, nice boundary and all-time liberating statement. It contains also a promise to receive suitable love in return, after you start giving suitably to another. Trust is mutual. Your own growth is parallel to the growth of another. Marvellous. You receive what you need by giving what you can.

Trust is a peculiar resource; it is built rather than depleted by use. (Unknown)

Vulnerable
Trust is thus also the willingness to be vulnerable to the reaction of someone else or the surroundings. That might feel like a big risk, because you are never sure of the response. After all, it doesn't have to be joyful, or even nice. When authentic, you slightly let go of complete control and dominance and learn to deal with the unexpected better in personal life and as manager. It's a case of OMM (Open Mind Management ... as the new term for authentic leaders).
So no more passively letting someone dominate your will, full of fear. Or to desperately try and say something sensible just to be accepted. By now, on the inside you know for sure that the unexpected will happen anyway and ... it's ok, it's welcome.

Then you can understand or accept it, bend it, shape it around or do something else positive with it. Then you will react with confidence and write just that little bit differently, like for instance: 'Dear client, thank you for this complaint!' or: 'Dear colleague, I have really noticed something positive in your curses, namely...!'

Dealing with that (with OMM) is not for everyone. A lot of people prefer a stark hierarchy, clear instructions, explicit guidelines and clearly defined times at which they can speak or act or work. They want to know what is expected of them (in advance). So when you, as their leader of chef, already expect that they do not expect anything that would be exactly what they were expecting of you. Such a measure of crystal clarity is just fine to all. Think of all those youngsters who are challenged by some autism or ADHD or PDD-Nos with their 'backpacks' who are soon to be working in, next to or are posted via your organization. Tell them to be creative and they will subsequently be very creative. When you expect them to be creative without voicing your expectations or without giving clear boundaries or instructions, it will all go horribly wrong with the mutual motivation.

> *Trust means renunciation control, and is in fact*
> *giving the other the opportunity to do what must be done,*
> *trusting (!) it will not be abused. (Paul Schnabel)*

When we see and feel that the other is up to his or her job or has mastered a skill and the organization supplies a matching service or product, our faith in his, her or it will grow. Especially if the sender succeed in communicating that in such a way, that it rises up to our expectations.

On our ruler of trust, what also counts is that we are able to compare earlier actions and behaviour that the new communication is credible and that words and deeds coincide.

Interest

One of the most important elements of corporate and personal authenticity is determining (whether by hearing, reading seeing, feeling, smelling or sensing) if the other party cares about you or the common interest. Literally and figuratively. Care, whether through use of time, money, deeds or actions. Intention and motivation, the ability to delegate and to let go and the open and honest way of communicating are the basic elements behind growing trust, and thus behind authenticity. To be stimulated you can already, while reading this, fill out a plus or a minus at a short summary of potential profits of trusts below. They are nice, soft words, which precede solid profits. So you can fill out a plus, if you think it will increase (thanks to giving trust) and a minus if you think it will decrease (by trusting). Here we go:

Motivation – Performance – Negotiations – Strong people – Tight organization – Loyalty – Commitment – Conformity – Problem solving ability – Conflict control – Satisfaction – Absence – Smooth processes – Acceptance of leadership – Accessibility - Right information – Pleasure – Ability to learn – Room for innovation – Flexibility

And? Filled out a lot of plusses? Then what are we waiting for?

How trust grows (again)

When the trust increases, it becomes stronger and the stronger it gets, the more valuable the experience becomes. Makes sense, right? At the start of a business relationship we often slyly give out trust away. We rationally calculate how the other person will behave in a situation in which we give away some trust and we anticipate the response if it is (not) returned. We mentally punish and reward ourselves in advance in order to make an identifiable base of trust and at the same time assess the advantages and disadvantages. Based on that we decide whether we stay or leave and whether the costs compensate the returns within this business (or personal) relationship. As time goes by the base of trust will grow, but only if both parties display visible, predictable and stabile behaviour, if deadlines are indeed made and if promises are kept. Predictability and reliability have to be experienced multiple times in order for them to be seen as a benefit or as something extra.

Deeper

When repetition of trustworthy behaviour conquers mutual acceptance the need to share values and norms, visions and goals with each other will automatically increase. This way, the mutual trust grows even further and slowly rises above the familiar, rational and cognitive components. The quality of the contact, the depth of the mutual interest then becomes more important than, for instance, the factual frequency of shipments or a tangible proof of, lets say, expertise.

When trust increases parties will more and more start to identify themselves with each other. Desires and intentions will be anticipated and half a word or look will be enough to understand each other, a shared culture is created. People sometimes understand each other so well, that they can speak or act on behalf of the other.

I often hear this – as a positive characteristic – in some relation-ships between management members: 'he /her has doesn't need more than half a word'. It often sounds like a reward or a wish.

> *Everything that irritates us about others can lead us towards an understanding about ourselves. (Carl Jung)*

Such a pity then, if it turns out to be one-way traffic, or just wishful thinking and the person in question interprets this 'half a word' it in an entirely different way. What despair and powerlessness it will produce, when one wants to communicate with half a word, and the other just doesn't get it at all and besides, doesn't know or feel what it is aimed at. Without mutuality, it just might as easily become manipulative behaviour and a deliberately created vagueness (no matter out of which motive for power, politics or personal insecurity) and that is not quite an authentic intention. What is missing here is the base of trust assumed present.

A better example of deep trust might be a couple that is married for a long time. For instance; he gives answers to questions someone else asks her and she agrees entirely with the answers he gives. Do you recognize that? The care for one another is complete, deep, strong and real. It is an emotional bond, which has dropped its anchors in the perception of care for each other, satisfaction of needs and unconditional attention, and therefore: blind trust.

Slow and quick
Woe betides, when trust is violated. Especially on an emotional level. The cooperation or the buying behaviour will collapse and people become mentally disable, get angry, unsatisfied, disappointed, and frustrated and avoid any contact. That does not bode well for the general atmosphere, planned efforts, vision based motivation and foreseen turnover.

The measure in which that happens and the speed with which it will become known and can be resolved is an important analysis for the leader or CEO in question (Mr. Toyoda himself climbed the stage, when the gas pedals in his US cars got stuck beginning 2010) and his head of PR. At least one of your seconds has to be there in advance in order to assess the perceptions of the outside world and make a more objective assessment of true facts versus possible emotions. Besides personal face validity, trust must also be regained from a business and profit point of view, but that probably won't come as a surprise.

During trust repair on a lower, more rational base without the deep emotional bond, the desired recovery will be more of an arithmetical problem of costs and returns, and therefore have the character of a material transaction. In that case it is all about the correct conclusion or handling of complaints, the right procedure, restitution, a fitting financial compensation or repair of what the outside world or the victim considers lost or failing in order to avoid nasty consequences or outcomes.

Sorry

The organization subsequently provides an explanation and is held responsible, illustrates the context in which it happened and that she sympathizes and is able to confirm the mixed feelings (of flawing). Think of the way supermarket chains or telecom providers handle things like that in Dutch shows like 'Radar'. During calamities within a relation with an already present bond of trust, next to genuine apologies, statement of regret and ample concrete measures for improvement are required as well in order to reinstate the balance of trust.

Concrete deeds are nearly as important, if not more important than words. But if the person communicating the message is not authentic (that means more than: seems authentic), or lacks the right face validity, and subsequently 'performs a theatrical play' (Tiger Woods' 'so sorry' speech with family and friends on TV early 2010), the damage and the implausibility only increases. Also think of the fall of the Dutch government whose ministers were busy texting in church about this, during the ongoing funeral of

Prince Claus (husband of queen Beatrix). I guess this kind of behaviour and priority setting, cost them dearly in terms of trust of and bonding with the Royal family.

> *There is always a way to be honest*
> *without being brutal. (Arthur Dobrin)*

Emotionally tight trusts ask even more of people when it's about a recovery operation. In that case those involved often conclude that the mutual base of common norms and values has been broken. That feels very serious and people even may get physically unwell. Think of adultery within a marriage or deceit of a clergyman, who has taken confessions for years in a row. It strikes quite the mental blow. A direct despair and severe doubt of someone's intentions, deeds and motives are the result ('I can't bear to be around him or her anymore') and people experience a form of treason of the mutual identity and unity once established together.

Removal

People don't wish to know someone anymore if this happens. Feelings of abandonment, alienation and removal are the result. Unfortunately, we probably all know an example in our direct surroundings, of ex lovers separating. For organizations and their network of relations and employees, it can have the same depth and severity (see my introduction and my own experience).

The director or owner or foreman in question (think of the Pope and the sexual abuse in the Roman Catholic Church) must offer their apology in person, quickly, voluntary and extensively, sincerely and profoundly. A clarification together with all the details and all the realization of damage repair and genuine promises might be fitting at this point. What also plays a part is another tangible confirmation of mutual commitment (think back to the texting minsters or the drama with Dutch skating coach Kemkers during the Olympics of 2010 when he robbed Sven Kramer of a certain golden medal) and an official, difficult promise to continue working together and remain loyal to the once agreed upon ideals and values.

> *It is not enough to know what is good;*
> *you must also be able to do it. (George Bernard Shaw)*

Communication from the heart and concrete commitments, actions and deeds, are of crucial importance here as well, for the restoration of a common, emotional bond (of trust) and relational focus for new results in the future.

Performance

There is never enough trust in the world and there is no point of trust saturation, it may and can always be more. But, like many times, a better world starts with you yourself as well. How do you give more trust? A useful summary for more growth of trust:

- *Communicate carefully, openly and transparently*
  Always be clear about your intentions, motives and always hold yourself responsible, when asked.
- *Try to show consistent and predictable behaviour*
  When you are consistent people will have an easier job of detecting if your words coincide with deeds and statements. Reduce the confusion about yourself, no matter how difficult.
- *Do your job professionally*
  Tasks and (social) engagements are preferably not a burden. Make sure that with everything you do, you really want to do it correctly.

- *Strengthen your integrity wherever possible*
    Keep your promises, whatever setbacks you encounter. Do what you've said you'd do. And: tell what you do and do what you tell.
- *Share and delegate responsibility*
    A leader gives his trust before he or she receives any. Let others think alongside you (also about crucial matters) and communicate what good this does all, or what you plan to do with it. Create a safe environment for colleagues or co-members to express their opinions.
- *Show your commitment*
    Be sensitive for the needs, wishes and interest of others. Respect them and help, wherever possible, realizing them, especially when they support the general 'values'. When you're working for no one but yourself, others will do the same.
- *Create a common identity*
    Sketch the future. Record what is of 'use and a necessity' and which expectations these two bring along. More We and You than Me and Someone. Bring people together more often (especially when they also work at home).
- *Formulate a vision with matching goals*
    What do we need to do and realize together? Emphasize the unity and every single person's unique role and contribution. Encourage people to listen to and learn from each other. Make mutual dependency more visible and tangible.
- *Strengthen values and the corporate appeal*
    Nowadays it's called Internal Branding. External promises (through buzz, networks, marketing and

communications) are just as important as all internal attention for them. In short, make 'inside' congruous to the 'outside'.

Sure, winning trust is a heroic act: you need to conquer yourself and take the risk that others violate that given trust. Trust is therefore an utterly humane, but dangerous merit. (Gerard Bodifee)

Consistent behaviour

Visible, consistent acting starts with keeping your promises and listening. When someone tells you something in good faith, and this person can keep that to himself, he at the very least trusts himself. That is the start for a base of trust with others. Trusting someone also means that you are able to let go of your urge to control and offer someone else the opportunity to do things that have to be done, after some kind of synchronization and consensus has been reached. Even if it goes somewhat wrong, it will eventually be alright, for there will remain trust in each other. There is more to be won than lost if we negotiate and act in good mutual trust. The measure of forgiveness (after errors or misunderstandings) is very much related to the measure of trust.

To be able to get closer to each other and make yourself the catalyst of more trust around you:

- *Do not judge, lest you be judged yourself*
    Let go of your own schedules and prejudice. Listen and be interested.
    No matter how hard this is
- *Speak from the heart, sincerely*
    Love the truth and let people know where they stand, display integrity and kindness and just forget the standard bla bla every now and then.

- *Show respect*
    Appreciate, honour and esteem the other. Look out for each other and keep others in mind, even if only because of qualities, performances and skills.
- *Create transparency*
    Explain what you are doing and make sure people are able to trace and verify this. What you see is what you get?
- *Rectify mistakes*
    Rectify yourself when you are wrong. Confirm someone else's feelings and emotions. Apologize correctly (preferably just a bit exaggerated). Remain modest.
- *Curiosity*
    Always keep improving yourself and always keep on learning. Ask for responses and act based on that feedback. Thank and praise others earlier and faster.
- *Recognize boundaries*
    Remain within the limits of your time, budget and promises. Do not make any promises you cannot hold and do not deliver inadequate performances on purpose. Do not make up excuses that YOU didn't start in time or didn't dare to. Tell them that YOU simply left too late … when you are late.
- *Confront reality*
    Highlight difficult subject and do not keep postponing them. Acknowledge what you sometimes do not say. Do not stick your head into the sand for too long. Recognize yourself and confess any performance anxiety or insecurities. Be strong with that thick (authentic) skin of yours and when people abuse you, let is slide away … it's their problem.

- *Take your own responsibility*

    Hold yourself responsible. Take responsibility for your mistakes, actions and results. Do not blame someone else and do not deprive yourself. Promise makes debt. Say what you do, listen before you talk too much. Want to know the other. Promise with words and act with actions.

Start converting any negative thoughts you've got about the business, the subject, yourself or the other, as much and as often as possible to positive ones. 'Just' don't allow yourself to think negative things...period!

Your own strength
Only compare yourself to yourself and never with a superficial other model, used as a frame of reference (from a magazine for instance). And when you look at others or want to imitate their behaviour, do so in order to learn from them. Look at what you are doing right. Again: focus on the good and not on the (inevitable and precious) mistakes. If need be, just make a list of positive items and results and read them regularly. Be open to and really enjoy the compliments you receive. Start giving well meant compliments yourself. You will feel better by doing so. Become pleasantly socially assertive. And learn to say no with a smile. If you make any mistakes, accept that you did so and take your responsibility. Always makes sure you keep on learning from your mistakes and setbacks, find and discover their (hidden) value.

Do not demand unrealistic thing of others and especially not of yourself. Make sure you meet the pre-arranged goals and don't make them too big or even entirely impossible to reach in advance. That way, enough breathing space will remain for you to authentically be of value to other people. Go do what you are good at, and where your strength lies. Find that out and allow yourself a test or training about it. Because you're working on things and matters you're good at, you'll automatically gain more faith and confidence. Find a number of positive people who already stimulate you by nature. And remember: passion attracts passion and conviction really works convincing. It's magical. The moment I made that known, that corporate authenticity became my item, new work relations with interesting people popped up at the spot on LinkedIn and via Twitter. Remarkable, is it not?

Systems and procedures

In order to produce a tangible result, some rules, procedures, protocols and agreements will (unfortunately) never cease to exist. This is because we want to minimize the risks and give people a reference. Too often, we fall back to the freedom-limiting reflex to make more rules, when something goes wrong. Rules like the Sarbanes Oxley (a law for companies who are stock market listed, or for foreign companies with an establishment in the US. The law aims to force decent management ethics and prevention of new scandals). The G20 countries together gave the Basel committee the assignment to find out how much cash the banks need to set aside as a safety net.

Rules, by themselves, will never inspire more trust. You need people who are willing to help fight the trap of not having to think for yourself (thanks to the rules and regulations). Why think and step down for a while? We have controls and checklists right? When the rules become more important than the (good) goal they were trying to accomplish, we have a major problem with our freedom, dependence and own responsibility as individuals.

On a side note: *as a test of my own free will and resistance against 'rules for rules', I sometimes scare my family. I once in a while drive through the red traffic light on purpose, but only if there isn't a single being, let alone a car or motorcycle in sight, whether left, right, in front of or behind the car. The commotion is brings about is huge. I, however, cannot cease to be amazed at the fact that we are apparently entirely conditioned to stop in front of a dumb red bulb, even if 'the reason why' is totally missing at that time.*

Trust only recovers (according to Van de Ven/ZBC) if living up to it coincides with an ability to judge accurately by executives and managers. When full attention is entirely given to the rules and certain things still go wrong (which always happens) that means that there is a pseudo-safety, which damages ones trust in organizations. We long for a system, which invites us to follow rules and processes if these, at the same time, stimulate us to display involved commitment and do not stifle and repress our behaviour. Rules and laws are here to serve people, not the other way around. End of story.

If results are quickly visible and the attention is focused on delivering performances for clients (so not just for colleagues alone) and attention is given to the question what people can contribute and how people can be of importance or meaning, this will automatically inspire job satisfaction, motivation and commitment in every echelon of the organization.

Too often have I observed management consultancy agencies that are asked to optimize the mutual cooperation between different departments, without focusing on and starting with: the buying customer or interested prospect or voting citizen outside the organization. Everyone has to understand the benefit and contribution of paying clients or strategic stakeholders. Only by realizing that, you will get constructive internal cooperation, meaningful focus and customer concentration while the dilemma between 'following rules' or 'risking trust' be conquered (in the favour of ... trust).

A lot of organizations have hidden away their rules and procedures in difficult to read texts. At the same time we expect more and more creativity, entrepreneurship and pro-activity from our highly trained employees and professionals. So why not adjust the procedures to those expectations? Speaking of expectations; I assisted several management teams in stimulating customer orientated and customer friendly behaviour amongst member of their staff. A lot of owners and entrepreneurs often do not get the fact that their people leave or even refuse to see so many opportunities for instant profit. My message is always: 'Dear CEO/owner, realize that if your employees were entrepreneurs, they wouldn't be in paid employment, but would've started for themselves'. So, while being busy optimizing internal co-operation, please improve that which is attainable and do not demand something that is impossible.

Attainable

The client generally expects 'operation excellence', and preferably at a price at which he cannot make or do it himself. The client expects a quality or creativity better than that of your competition and expects a reliability in conformity with that which was promised to him (and preferably a bit more). Can we attain that by introducing more systems or by starting to trust each other more, in these rough economic times?

> *The companies that survive longest are the one's that*
> *work out what they uniquely can give to the world*
> *not just growth or money but their excellence, their respect for*
> *others, or their ability to make people happy. Some call those*
> *things a soul. (Charles Handy)*

Operations excellence also depends on the strategy, targets plus the contribution, creativity and the initiatives of the different teams and departments. Therefore, use summarizing 'dashboards' as top manager in order to monitor, compare and judge figures and numbers daily. And use the time you gain with these ICT systems, for improved approachability and creating more room to innovate and improve. Select creative people, so they can develop means and measures to limit mistakes and shortcomings. Combine parameters for tangible performance and factual behaviour with achieving 'soft' goals or mission policies. Connect people to the processes they invented them selves or to mutually developed measures, means and regulations (of control). This way, governance, risk management and compliance are related to a human scale and become recognisable practices. And that is enjoyable and fruitful for everyone.

Cancel all those needless controls and, especially, that senseless supervision. When too many people are doing detention-like work in prison-like buildings, completing dull checklist, we will all go bankrupt together one day. Non-productive activities limit our power to compete. Temporarily scratch a rule and see what happens (in some cities red traffic-lights are turned off at Sunday morning 05.30 hrs, thankfully). Let the entrepreneur's type and other employees figure it out together. Create mixed teams with the right different characters to innovate. And keep those European bureaucrats at a distance and do not pleasure them by our devoted, goody and sometimes panting exemplary behaviour as Dutchmen, for such an attitude isn't really working to our advantage.

A little bit of civil disobedience is hard to discover in The Netherlands anyhow, where compliance, acting 'normal' and safety in the norm. Try to dare people into looking over their fences. Give trust and compliments. In a country where 'being normal is crazy enough', we should appreciate to 'stand out of the crowd' more.

People don't mind being part of a group, if only they still have an individual say. So your employees still want to have the feeling that they are a part of a family, but only if everyone actually listens to each other. Tight, top down hierarchies are done for because they kill the fun factor and the motivation for an extra effort. Research shows that performance increases when the initiative of employees are made crucial. At the same time, that makes many old school managers uncertain. For them, nothing will really be as it was before. The crucial thing to hold on to is an authentic YOU. Less and less authentic people have to rely on the certainty of others, the past or on creativity limiting regulations. That is the new economic reality. This goes for individuals as well as organizations. If your stick to yourself authentically, you are able to maintain yourself in times of great changes and keep helping others and coach the content, arguments, benefits and visions.

Google

Let us be inspired by Google a little? Quotes from the Google website (8/2010):

> 'Google is not a conventional company, and we don't intend to become one. True, we share attributes with the world's most successful organizations – a focus on innovation and smart business practices comes to mind – but even as we continue to grow, we're committed to retaining a small-company feel. At Google, we know that every employee has something important to say, and that every employee is integral to our success. We provide individually tailored compensation packages that can be comprised of competitive salary, bonus, and equity components, along with the opportunity to earn further financial bonuses and rewards.

Google:

10 reasons to work for us

1. Lend a helping hand. With millions of visitors every month, Google has become an essential part of everyday life – like a good friend – connecting people with the information they need to live great lives.

2. Life is beautiful. Being a part of something that matters and working on products in which you can believe is remarkably fulfilling.

3. Appreciation is the best motivation, so we've created a fun and inspiring workspace you'll be glad to be a part of, including on-site doctor; massage and yoga; professional development opportunities; shoreline running trails; and plenty of snacks to get you through the day.

4. Work and play are not mutually exclusive. It is possible to code and pass the puck at the same time.

5. We love our employees, and we want them to know it. Google offers a variety of benefits, including a choice of medical programs, company-matched 401(k), stock options, maternity and paternity leave, and much more.

6. Innovation is our bloodline. Even the best technology can be improved. We see endless opportunity to create even more relevant, more useful, and faster products for our users. Google is the technology leader in organizing the world's information.

7. Good company everywhere you look. Googlers range from former neurosurgeons, CEOs, and U.S. puzzle champions to alligator wrestlers and Marines. No matter what their backgrounds, Googlers make for interesting cube mates.

8. Uniting the world, one user at a time. People in every country and every language use our products. As such we think, act, and work globally – just our little contribution to making the world a better place.

9. Boldly go where no one has gone before. There are hundreds of challenges yet to solve. Your creative ideas matter here and are worth exploring. You'll have the opportunity to develop innovative new products that millions of people will find useful.

10. There is such a thing as a free lunch after all. In fact we have them every day: healthy, yummy, and made with love'.

Smaller units
While searching for alternatives (within the current economic system) for the big, current, unauthentic and often paralyzing complex and hierarchal organizations, two familiar alternatives are stumbled upon. One: the splitting cells alternative, according to Dutchman Eckart Wintzen. This pioneer, thinker and entrepreneur (his legacy lives on through Extent.nl) had the vision as well as the guts to build a successful IT organization based on small, independent units or cells. The formula is one of extensive delegations of responsibility. It is not only model, it's also a way of thinking and doing and a management philosophy. In the end, it all comes down to trust.

His point of view: why all the excessive control? You hire someone for a specific spot because you have faith in his abilities, right? Trust him then! Tell people they themselves are allowed to achieve their goals and have to keep an eye on the rationality of them themselves.

Only strength can co-operate.
Weakness can only beg. (pres. Dwight Eisenhower)

65

Conformity to the rules and the system are often more important than the output. Every cell director at Wintzens' BSO was offered free decision room around a few clear targets and only a few rules to run his own 'cell company', hire his own staff, acquire his own assignments, lease his own cars, organize team trips and so on. When a cell had more than 65 employees, it had to be split into two new cells. From their own circle of employees, the staff had to elect a new manager. That way, two single cells moved on with each 30 staff members etc. According to Wintzen this model worked, because it simply gave responsibility to people within some general guidelines.

Letting go

Furthermore the organization did not know any staff departments, for the cells organized their own management. That meant no classic branched organizational structures (a la Mintzberg). One risk is/was the chance of a battle for the same customer (which would be fought by cells among each other. Also, prospects asked the same quotation at different cells, to compare and let them compete one against the other) and the hiring of too much staff. Important principle of this model was the fact that you took a new fresh look at traditional habits (you automatically develop through time as cell director). Think of status, power, invisibility, increased distance from the working floor and getting parted from 'the real customer outside'. How the goals were reached within each different cell was entirely up to them. You would leave that to the 65 men staff and every cell could have a different approach.

There is, however, a catch there. You have to be willing, as a leader, to step back from being the single person dictating how everything should be managed and you have to be able to accept, even with some admiration or pleasure, that someone else runs things entirely different. We are so used to taking control ourselves upon encountering problems and 'quickly' solving them at once. Building small cells or units, within bigger layers, may be a future answer to the impossible increase of scale and span of control. What follows is alienation from everything we once regarded as 'the human scale'. No matter how subjective determining hat scale is.

The co-operation
The co-operation is a second, quite remarkable model, in the wake of the era of uncontrolled ego capitalism and self-enrichment. Think of the co-operate Rabobank, which is escaping (for now?) the banking crisis (which came into being because of the IOU's, derivatives and all sorts of vague, collateral financial products and mortgages) thanks to their (forced) carefulness. At the Rabobank, the local banks, the members, are in charge. They work together with (and sometimes fight) the central HQ management that only takes initiative if it benefits every local bank and, especially, the customer.

By joining the purchases, PR and IT, they create economies of scale and spread the risks. By regarding each other as members and not as competitors, sharing knowledge, people and 'best practices' is almost self-evident. Product development or a combined loyalty program for customers produces synergy, recognition and surplus value, but cannot go at the expense of independence or the suffrage of the members.

> *If you want to be incrementally better: Be competitive.*
> *If you want to be exponentially better: Be cooperative.*
> *(Unknown)*

The co-oporation belongs to the members and serves the members. They all benefit from the right services for the right prices and all may have a say in the matter. It keeps the central management focussed and alert. But, the management structure can possibly be paralyzing as well, or produce inertia. There has to be enough space to undertake things locally or decentralized. It relies on balancing the individual and common interest. That requires a lot of deliberation and communication and may lead to a loss of momentum and decisiveness. For the coming 20 years it might turn out to be a profitable structure. And, in hindsight, maybe the total lack of decisiveness was a welcome change from the 'total madness' on the financial markets. Who is to say, it is still too early to praise the Rabobank, seen as the crisis still rages on. Besides, the co-oporation as a model had been known for a long time and is also successfully used in Dutch healthcare, agriculture and housing sectors.

> *If you want to build a ship, don't herd people together to collect wood and don't assign them tasks and work, but rather teach them to long for the endless immensity of the sea. (Antoine de Saint-Exupéry)*

Human scale

The underlying need for a different model is that of the new authentic human scale, in which we rediscover the commitment to each other, the company, the trade and the goal. New applications of the internet also help. Co-thinking, co-versation and co-creation helps innovations and speeds up repair packs or damage control measures thanks to online platforms. 'Crowd Sourcing' is an useful forerunner of that. The goal is to help develop or improve a product by means of a real, open and thus authentic dialogue between, for instance, the manufacturer and the consumer. Daring to let go of the reins and learning to give or share is, apparently, an important condition of more loyal customer/employee/stakeholder /organization relationships in the future.

It has yet to come at that in politics and management. Most people still expect leadership from their leaders. The political party of Dutch politician Rita Verdonk, TON (2008), once wanted to let the public co-compose their political program. A good idea in theory, but it turned out 'the public' wasn't ready for it yet and proved to be too a variegated partner to develop and do business with. The new authentic leader will have to keep drawing boundaries, formulating a vision and policy, coaching and communicating the rules of the game and focus as well as bundle the results. 'The top' however, still has the privilege of taking the final decision, and of course it will always stay that way. But I would rather see it set in a smaller, flatter hierarchical pyramid, where we know and respect the woman or man making the final choices and to whom we can go to with our problems, than in the detached, incomprehensible dictate of a 'not my problem' leader or board of directors, management or council.

6.

The Yield Factor: Credibility

Good, effective and productive relationships are preferably built on a quantity of proven or supposed trust and on credibility. Credibility is essential in every business transaction. And: every CEO, manager, salesmen, politician and administrator will want to be, stay or become credible.

Credibility is the conclusion, which was made from experience and confirmed trust in the relationship with a person or organization. It has objective (confirmed shipments, repeated trustworthiness and predictability) and subjective (atmosphere, image, culture) elements.

Expertise is definitely a part of this, but this is both objective as well as subjective and therefore hard to fully incorporate.

Entirely subjective are the criteria for credibility like charisma, enthusiasm, passion and (physical) appeal. They're all elements playing their part and weaken or strengthen our idea of credibility.

Pyramid

Graham Jones developed a model by which you'll really become credible, provided you reach the top after going through the first four layers:

Bottom layer 1: 10% is knowledge

At the bottom lies knowledge. Surprisingly enough it only contributes 10% to your credibility, but you cannot do without. No knowledge and you'll make a mess and go down the drain. There goes your credibility!

Middle layer 2: 15% is focus

That means that it is crucial to consistently put your knowledge on display, thus explicitly. A prospect or relation wants clarity and intelligible explanation and language. Communicate your knowledge in a way, which fits the other.

Middle layer 3: 25% is passion

Enthusiasm is very important. It accounts for at least 25%. People able to show more passion in their message are regarded as more credible. That might not be fully objective, but it's the truth. Shy and introverted organizations and managers have the disadvantage (and now got hold of a personal target!).

Top layer 4: 50% is commitment

This is the top layer. 50% of your credibility depends on your commitment. You have to be involved with your surroundings and employees. Empathy is important. Show your citizens, clients and colleagues you care about them.

Nearly every leader active in our economic and politic social system has a message, product and an idea or wants to share knowledge. An important conclusion of the pyramid is, that the knowledge component often receives too much attention, and the commitment too little, especially in bigger organizations.

If you seek to bond or get in contact with buyers and consumers, show your commitment. This is what is increasingly missing in our egocentric age and will call for a new fulfilment when we can (or must) remove the ego madness or uncontrolled greed from our current system.

> *The more you are willing to accept responsibility for*
> *your actions, the more credibility you will have.*
> *(Brian Koslow)*

Same as trust?

Credibility is the trust others have in your capacity to provide results (and keep providing results). Trust is the faith other have in you, based on your integrity. Trust is the more personal of the two (credibility being the second) and the most elusive. It has to do with the feelings of vulnerability, confirmation, appreciation and responsibility towards others.

Trust isn't necessarily a requirement for credibility. As a leader, you are able to provide a professional and consistent result, without having a base of trust. But to be trusted credibility and expertise is nearly always essential. The difference is often the most obvious when observing political foremen. Dutch CDA minister Maxime Verhagen (or any other, for that matter) is capable, educated and credible, but isn't trusted by a (large) part of the population. For a different part, he might be trusted, but not credible. Do you notice the difference?

It'll be clear that it's all much related, and is often combined. One definition states, for instance, that credibility is the measure in which leaders inspire trust with the people depending on their leadership, by following up on promises and by giving tangible information (quote from: woorden.nl). Or it is the measure in which a person deserves to be trusted (wiktionary.com). Or credibility is: authenticity, reliability and goodwill (mijnwoorden-boek.nl).

Indispensible

Credibility is an important characteristic, simply because it stimulates trust. Very useful for every CEO, manager and executive so that he is able to involve people and get things done quicker, with more support.

> *Credibility is like virginity. Once you lose it,*
> *you can never get it back. (Unknown)*

Just like charisma, credibility is a characteristic, which others reward you with and which you earn back, as it were, through feedback and responses. You want more credibility? Then you'll have to change something in people's opinions. They have to start thinking differently about you or your organization. It might require an image, advertising, communication campaign, TV commercials or PR spin, but that is not (or no longer) enough. Becoming, being and showing your authenticity is, from now on condition 'numero uno' for credibility during the coming twenty years!

Performance and vigor are, of course, a part of that, just like intention and words. Saying and showing always go together.

Crucial points for credibility

1. *Show a sense of direction.* Let people know what you're going and are standing for. Not everyone has to agree with you, but be clear and precise.
2. *Behave consistently.* If you give your opinion, don't change it the next moment. If you adjust your opinion do so after due deliberation and motivated. Don't change it too often!
3. *Steadfastness.* Let employees know what your beliefs and values are. Do not follow every hype just because you think this will help you get more sympathy.

4. *Adjust your words to your behaviour.* Congruence in what you say, write and do is very important. Preferably harmony is present between making a promise and also keeping it. Never let promises water down. You will always be reminded of it. Do what you stand for. Always take the initiative when you have to break you promises and explain why you can't keep them.

5. *A deal is a deal.* If you agree upon something with your colleagues, know that are counting on you to hold up your end of the deal. Preferably, everyone should live up to his or her promises. Prevent people's (continuing) resistance. Appeal to people's responsibility. Don't participate in endless discussions about choices that were already made and can be obvious.

6. *The stereotyping.* No matter how unique and individual you are, in order to come across credible, it always comes in handy to allow relations or colleagues to stereotype you. Do not give the impression that your personal style might be entirely different tomorrow, compared to today.

Selfishness is not living as one wishes to live, it is asking others to live as one wishes to live. (Oscar Wild)

7. *Transparency.* Nourish the idea that you have nothing to hide. That is, of course, very relative, for 'deep down', we all have something to hide. The way the personal CEO communicates is often very smart and strategically calculated. That might change towards a more tactical communication (not clumsy or naïve, but more 'vulnerable'). If you aren't willing to do such a thing, realize then that you're 'visible' and have a high profile offline, as well as online.

8. *Become an open book.* That takes guts. And by showing

this courage, you'll increase your credibility. Moreover, a certain measure of self-disclosure also brings about an open response and feedback. Naivety isn't a desired, logical extension either.

9. *Let yourself and your organization be heard and seen.* Invisibility gives the impression that there is something to hide. Anonymity makes unpopular. Learn to confront and make time for your constituency, followers, employees and family members. Know your facts by heart.

10. *Be authentic.* Continue to be yourself while making choices, and especially while communicating those choices. People know your values, especially in an impersonal environment where they might get the impression of manipulation.

Everything that is real, sincere and true is a refreshing revelation. Please, never become a copy of someone. Remain authentic and in motion. Continue to learn and change, your authenticity isn't static either, and never 100% finished.

Reputation

Help build a (new) reputation from the inside out. So no longer the reputation created for you by agencies, spin doctors or campaigns. The new proof of credibility is authenticity, on a personal, as well as organizational level. Any organization has (or even is) a personality. Including 'character', moods, senses and cycles. Accepting this is the very basis of my hypotheses that if we as individuals can become authentic, so can any organization that is made out of hundreds or thousands of individuals. Because 'the small part' represents 'the whole unity'. Does the Irisscopist see your body and even mental condition in (one of) your eyes as mirroring your soul? Even the soles of your feet show all there is to know about your health and energy fields?

This insight might provide you (sorry: your organization) with a reputation that is resilient, trustworthy and is believable.

If you allow some level of accessibility and approachableness, people will learn to know you and just by doing that, people will become more positive about you or the organization, which you stand for. That, subsequently, has a positive effect on others, and so on and so forth. Having faith in your own abilities increases the trust in you, or your organization, especially when modesty also comes into play and recognition of the Universal Power Source that inspired that result. Other building stones for your credibility are up for grabs, really. Like: Be honest and don't lie (if need be, make a selection of the available information or remain silent). When people find out the ugly truth (which always happens, sooner or later) all your credibility will be lost. Show your trust in others (you measure your corn by the bushel). You're only credible if you have faith in (the performances of) others. In a while, the way you do things will make that clear to others, in your smile, eyes and attitude as well.

Credible brands

The difference between credible brands or persons (or institutions and organizations) isn't all that big, for the principles are, for a large part, the same. Brands also rely on trustworthiness, willingness (to deliver and take responsibility) and expertise (through explanation, supplying information and image). The benefit of credible brands is that the company can easily put its own price + on it and new developments can be introduced at 'a head start'. The consumer is willing to pay more for credibility and will grant you more goodwill. This does, however, require consistent behaviour, aura and continuing investment in a mix of authentic marketing (including goals like presence and visibility).

Think of Dutch brands like Douwe Egberts coffee and her shops and products, such as tableware and coffee machines, which all have a lot of added value for the credibility of the parent company, helped by consistent 'branding' and investments in the market, which has been going on for decades. Naturally, roasting good coffee comes first and subsequently functional and trustworthy goods come second. The same way a person, for instance a CEO, without even the most basic knowledge (comes first), will not make in on the ruler of credibility.

Consumers with a choice and any feeling of indecisiveness will be hugely stimulated by the credibility of the service or the product and especially ... the personality of the sender. This way, strong relationships are forged over time: the accumulation of credibility signs and signals by means of a calculated mix of media usage and consistent, recognizable messaging.

Peter Blackshaw summarizes it in a beautiful and concise way in his arrangement of six parameters for the acquirement of credibility in the new, social and online media environment:

1. Trust

Certainty, consistency, integrity and authority.

2. Authenticity

Genuineness, sincerity, informality and keeping promises.

3. Openness

Attainability, open doors and windows, accessibility, presence and no secrets.

4. Conformation

Constantly repeating, improving search results, participation and justifying online communities, feedback of third parties (forums).

5. Listening

Ability to sympathize, modesty, warm welcoming, asking for and settling feedback.

6. Feedback
Speed, accuracy, recovery actions and measures, responding to changes, handling complaints.

Changes

In daily business practices change and resistance to change is an inconvenient and often psychological matter. Organizations often work with a lot of methods, protocols and strategies and often hire external agencies, which put the employee, the process or the strategy in the centre of change. Employees are involved through workshops, sessions and trainings, sometimes at a childish and downright insulting level. People do want to change, but do not want to be changed. Nearly never are their problems and desires taken into account, is the credibility of their leaders questioned or are they asked if they themselves really want to be a part of the changes. If you have are an authentic, credible leader, this alone and almost instantly results in large leaps forward in any change process. They 'emit' the information and communication from the start. They do not spend it on an external agency or HRM department. No, they participate and ensure a credible realization and, if need be, a succession or successor.

Need and necessity

Managers and leaders are the ones who should know and are able to tell employees about the need and necessity of a new course or any adjustment of an existing one. Why is that forgotten so quickly! Many already think they are doing useful work when they're just managing 'the processes'. Ha. They are not, however, real front man, but just shop attendants or, at the most, behave like middle managers. Credible leaders make substantiated arguments and have a very loyal bond with their organization. Leaders without, or with less credibility, need a longer time for a change of structure, culture or course. You, yes you just look around today and pick someone from inside your council, team or management and decide who is most capable of pulling the cart from this change perspective? Are there any people left? Is it you? Do you come forward, take the word and lead the troops? Chrysler Motors got better through the performance of Lee Iacocca in her TV Advertising. Steve Jobs = Mr. Apple. They give a different meaning to the letters CEO, namely Clarity, Explanation and Openness (source unknown). Take it as an example please.

> Try not to become a man of success but rather try to become a man of value. (Albert Einstein)

Stability, involvement, reassurance and 'face validity'; that's what it's all about in times of change and modern leadership. People will be mobilized earlier and better by leaders with an authentic tone of voice, conviction, inner strength, commitment and especially emotional singularity, stability and purity. This is quite close to the list of characteristics for authenticity. Employees follow and show enthusiasm for leaders who mean every word they say and act in our interest for the good of all.

Emotion
Authentic credibility is made up from content and an emotional, social side. Content wise there are rational arguments, which have the unique benefit of underlining e.g. the profit figures or the sales efforts. The emotional input is provided by the person himself, his or her character and enthusiasm, the vision, the keeping of promises, making the right choices, stepping in when people are frustrating, the ability to communicate a sense of urgency and relate efforts to tangible successes.

> Attitude is a little thing that makes a big difference. (Winston Churchill)

Reorganizations and reductions in expenditure (take note Dutch government of 2010/2011) are often founded by a promise of extra benefit later on. Fine, but in reality people often get little or nothing in return and both fragmentation and compromises subsequently weaken the personal credibility of the messenger. Consequently people have even less faith in promised returns in the next period after the disillusive one, let alone offer their cooperation or obedience. When vision, drive, trust and faith are missing from the start, it's time for a change of CEO (or prime minister) to try to save the day for a needed reorganization or change.

Self-employed

With little to no national exposure, it's harder for a small entrepreneur to display credibility. Still, on the whole, the same rules that apply to the big leaders, also apply to the small leaders. Treat your customers, suppliers and employees with respect; pay them on time and not too late or little on purpose. Listen to their wishes and do something about them, either directly or indirectly. Make sure they become ambassadors to your company and speak well of you, your company or organization. What certainly helps is paying your bills sooner than is indicated on the invoice. This way, you make 'friends with the Mammon' and make it a PR instrument, It ensures that your suppliers will go through fire for you later on, and are wiling to put in an extra effort when needed.

Admit your mistakes and remain reasonable when they complain or misunderstood. Maybe admit them just a bit sooner than you feel you should admit them. Solve separate matters in separate ways. Realize that people talk a lot more than you think about your company and the way you perform. Do not underestimate the power of testimonials (on the website, blog, bulletins or in adverts). Buying space for advertisement is always possible but cheaper relevant quotes of clients are extremely important for any new relation or customer. Remain stable and in control and only lose your patience at home or in the sauna please.

You ARE the company. It's as simple as that.

Cost control

In order to acquire some trust and increase your reputation, a few cheap tips will be given:

1. *Become a guest speaker: (locally/regionally, for a school, Network Group or club).* You never know who's listening, even if there doesn't seem to be any prospects at first sight. Distribute handouts of your contribution (not an ego speech please) and a business card. Ask for the list of participants and send a little something extra to them for free (a book, gimmick or an article or something, a sample or thirty minutes of your time for free).
2. *Do some charity work:* it shows your commitment and it is a welcome change. Only do it for something, which is related to you (whether personally or professionally). This way, others get the change to appreciate you more, or find you more likeable. People just rather do business with someone they know and like. Simple fact. Even if you have doubt, you'll get the best feedback and advice while doing volunteer work. Because it's about you, there isn't any business drive on you; it's about you as a person/human being, and not as a politician or director. Who knows, it might even draw some local media attention!
3. *Have the courage to give something away:* Donate to charity or organize an event or lecture yourself. Write articles and supply comments. In the local newspapers or carefully selected online forums. Realize that a reward or feedback might take a while and doesn't instantly result in more turnover or profit made. Do not be discouraged when you don't get any reactions.

Behind the screens you enjoy being an authentic personality, and when the time is right, the mail or call carrying your long-awaited new business request resulting from e.g. your Google Adwords campaign, will come. The secret for this being your sincere interest and time and attention given to others voluntarily. If you're only present to look for new clients, if often will work against you. See it as an opportunity to help others without any strings attached, who knows what will happen (and if nothing happens, at least it was pleasant). 'Just' do people favours. I was once asked to be an auctioneer at a fundraiser for a refugee project. People thought: "You're in PR right? Then I bet you're a good talker". I had never done it before and I certainly didn't see any way to earn some doe. I did it anyway. First off, it was exceptionally fun (I raised a lot) and … I got 2 assignments within three months out of it.

4. *Start blog and share information.* Write your own articles or collect information/articles of others (with links and mention sources). Take care not to copy whole stretches of text written by someone else and do not forgot to share your perspective, opinion or judgment on the matter. Offer tips and attract attention like: Three steps to prepare you for… or: Seven ways to spend money more smartly … etc.
5. *Let yourself be seen and heard and 'do never fear people's judgment'.* Link your blog to your social network and address files and your website and thus create synergy and a cycle of relevance. Stay close to your profession. Building credibility as a vicar, while you're in construction might become confusing for readers and relations.

Some have it …

Think of a meeting where a new participant comes up with an idea, which is recognized, as useful by everyone present.

Because they got stuck before. The amount of credibility explodes at the spot, because everyone believes this idea of yours is extremely sensible. Even better: propose a meeting where you propose to bring someone else in, because he might have experience on that subject or he knows someone else who knows a lot about it. You instantly become more credible because of his supposed (loaned) experience or knowledge of the other person. It isn't for nothing that people use the credibility-increasing trick to mention names of other well-known people they supposedly know in front of a new conversation partner.

Example: 'Oh, so you must know Jack X, who also works in your branch?' or: 'Did you work at Firm C? Then you must know director G who later on did business with me and F?' The trick behind it is that you have to say NO (tsss ... like you care who those people are), but that the credibility of the one with, apparently, so many relationship and contacts increases on the spot. He rises in your esteem. And it so happens that is entirely the point. This is, however, not an authentic method if there is somehow any conscious tactics involved. By the way: you can read more about manipulation in the upcoming chapter 'Communication'.

If someone doesn't really have any names ready for use or has a large network at his disposal, it might take a bit longer to become credible in the eyes of others. In that case it's important to regularly show that you really are 'worthy' of one's 'trust and faith'. By, for instance, repeatedly rise up to expectations or by delivering on multiple occasions, that which you promised. Just as long until people say: 'That person, he can be counted on!'.

... some don't anymore
You can, alas, lose credibility as well. When you slowly gained it, it can be lost again quite quickly.

People loose their credibility and podium just like that. Any normal event can entirely change the general perception of someone and to his disadvantage. It doesn't even require a blunder or something big. The credibility of a CEO will e.g. fall almost simultaneously with the market value of his company. One year you're the hero, the other you are the loser. Ask soccer trainers.

That way you can see how relative the perception of others really is. Leaders who fell, once had a large number of followers. They used to think strategically about these things, the time of person brand building (a profession in its own right): 'What characteristics do 'they' want to see of me now? What do 'they' want to hear today of me? Which style will I perfect to get status? Who are my preferred followers tomorrow? Which characteristics do they appreciate and how will I twist and play with their beliefs and trust?'

> *Love all, trust a few, do wrong to none.*
> *(William Shakespeare)*

It was the time of putting on masks, use false information, twist the facts and hide the truth and use Machiavellian power play. Macho attitudes and egoistic motives and manipulation elevated to a form of art. That time of war with yourself has passed. You are credible in the eyes of others, but preferably in your own eyes first.

Integrity

In order to become credible as a leader and a human being, integrity is especially needed. Your inside and outside are balanced. Your values coincide with your behaviour. That sometimes proves to be a difficult combination. Acting upright is also the acceptance of the fact that we just happen to make mistakes, and that we learn from those mistakes. Only when we aren't able to learn from our mistakes anymore (and we don't want to learn from them), is there a serious credibility issue.

> *It is hard to believe that a man is telling the truth when you know that you would lie if you were in his place.*
> *(Henry Louis Mencke)*

What is so hard about confirming what everyone can see and knows about all along: You were wrong! A family man, who admits his vulnerability, wins the love of his children. He shows that he is aware of his conscience, his emotional life and those of others. I have met senior managers who admitted that the uttering of even an (tiny) apology was simply 'not done', even though they knew they were wrong. It was simply not an issue for these leaders, because it would make them look 'weak'. Unbelievable!. Who told them that? How far from the truth can you be?

If a well-known leader knows that 'everyone' (the press, for instance) is going to tear him apart tomorrow, maybe that tells us more about the press than about the credibility of the leader in question. Authentic leaders don't need to blame someone else or the media nor the circumstances or feel to justify themselves afterwards, or trivialize the situation and their choices made. They win their authority by taking their responsibility and are able to control their own image and perception processes. He himself is the new moral authority where, by now, the whole nation or organization yearningly is waiting for or looking forward to these days of spiritual poverty.

Qualities
Integrity presumes the presence of pure qualities such as a feeling for harmony and unity, consistence, honesty, innocence, purity and uprightness and the absence of lying, cheating or stealing. *Honesty* has a lot to do with the measure of acting, upholding and

communicating the norms and values of religion (Christianity has a strong urge for honesty stemming from the ten biblical commandments/guidelines to properly live together). Besides, honesty has nothing, or at least less, to do with heredity and, as such, is not an innate virtue (red: taken from an article in The Economist).

> *Sometimes I wonder whether the world is being run by smart people who are putting us on, or by imbeciles who really mean it. (Mark Twain)*

Moral responsibility is the consequence of fulfilling your promise, commitment or performance. When you retract a clear commitment, you are responsible for the replacement. If you're not able to do so, you are morally responsible for the emotional damage someone else contracts. Dutch minister Wouter Bos was the moral and ethical winner concerning the commitment The Netherlands made to withdraw from Afghanistan (2009/2010).

Sincerity is the virtue of talking about your feelings, thoughts and desires. Despite the risks of vulnerability and, thus, abuse, we expect sincerity from our loved ones, examples and idols. Professor Charles Norton points out that sincerity from morality preceded the modern notion of authenticity. No matter how hard it is to grip yourself, he explains is as: being faithful to yourself.

It is time to find out what's that all about.

> *All credibility, all good conscience, all evidence of truth come only from the senses (Friedrich Nietzsche)*

7.

Authenticity

Has it finally been enough then, living and working under the false appearances of happiness and the fake images of ideals fed to you by controlled media? Or the white collar greed and corruption, the abuse of power and the humiliation of people being exploited?

The poignant economic slavery and dishonesty, stimulated by artificial scarcity and maximum pursuit of money through profit by 'growing, expanding and growing, expanding' is inevitably coming at her end because of the economy of credit and debt breaking down. The fight to hold on just a bit longer is still raging in full, here in the West anno 2010. The 'powers that be' will keep having their way, if need be through decay of living standards, child labor or, eventually, through war and massive destruction of everything that is valuable.

The Western world governments as our Big Brother is installing even more monitoring systems, scans, checkpoints, supervision and regulations enabling the rise of the one strong opposition leader (after which fascism will be reborn). The resistance to authority, polarization of opinions and sense of discontent amongst the people is growing, and counter-movements are getting more support.

Slowly, but surely, we awaken and realize that the current system of trade and society is trembling on her postwar foundations. That is, if we still know what those foundations actually were (something like: living together is not living apart and resisting the attitude of 'me, myself and I and less for you and we').

Desire for genuineness
Trust and natural authority because of ascendency or wisdom have been lost to leaders for so long, that we might even start to think that it was all planned this way by a group of power hungry individuals behind the stage. A lot of people are slowly getting enough of this and are counting on a peaceful transition towards a more sincere, dignified and authentic society, where 'freedom' is more than just a catchphrase, but where it can actually be lived.

The beginning of change is serving through genuine sincerity and for an appeal on everyone's responsibility in shared dependence and authenticity. End fake; embrace real. Questions:
- When did you last eat a tomato, grown the way it should've grown, without form or color manipulation and added chemical flavoring?
- When did you last speak with someone, from heart to heart without fear for ... all sorts of things?
- How did it come to be that you prefer the smell of gasoline, above that of a farm?
- Where do specialized builders still lay bricks to build an ageless, refined and decorated façade, out of love for 'what is possible' and for lasting beauty, instead of mathematically adjusting prefab elements, coming directly from the factory.
- Who told you that you are more attractive, if you first started to look like some celebrity from a TV show (and why do you want that?)

Leaders have now invented the "preventative" warfare.
We are now starting a Middle East war, in order
to prevent a possible war. We now sow death,
in order to forestall death. (Jan Marijnissen, Dutch politician)

- When did you last realize that it is your money with which governments bail out banks for hundreds of billions of euro's and pay their hundreds of thousands officials.
- Why does a leader, who reads out loud some pre-fabricated story, which includes even the pauses and the hand gestures, appeal to you?
- When did you really believe a 100% profit-oriented multinational, which, based on the same old combustion engine, produces a so-called 'environmentally friendly or even green car'?
- How did you find out that the rising and falling exchange rates on stock markets, have little to do with the honest trade based on supply and demand between 'real' companies?
- When did you last see pain, human hardship and suffering in a 'real life' TV soap?
- How fake are online relationships with people you never met in person, based on made up profiles and false names (because of which even genuine offline relationships go to pieces)?
- How much time did it last take you to really think about something (your own life for instance) and have an opinion about something, without parroting your (opinion) leader?
- When did you last visit a smaller shop with a different collection of goods, rather than the standard and uniform shops behind standard facades located in almost standardized shopping streets?

- When did you consciously take distance from the marketed need for 'bigger!', 'more!' or 'new!' or 'buy now!' and did you feel as victor and 'in control'?

Are you still able to know, feel, smell, hear and find out what is real and what is fake, what is false and pretence and what is of lasting value and beauty? I won't answer that, you probably already know.

Old World

Earlier on I wrote about primal emotions such as fear and hope. Two provocative additions:
1. Fear is good. Fear keeps you sharp. Fear makes you take the next step and makes sure adrenaline is produced at the right moments, useful for not dying in life threatening situations. Fear makes sure you vote wisely. So let us be afraid and let that fear rule you. Fear is the new happiness of the 21st century and it warns you about something new.
2. The point is that greed, for lack of a better word, is good. Greed is right, greed works. Greed clarifies, cuts through, and captures the essence of the evolutionary spirit. Greed, in all of its forms; greed for life, for money, for love, knowledge has marked the upward surge of mankind. And greed, you mark my words, will not only save your company but also that other malfunctioning corporation called The Western World. (Loosely quote Gorden Gekko).

They are paradigms of the old world. Of course fears are also survival instincts saving humans. Fear, as well as greed has, strangely enough, brought a lot of good, in danger or poverty. If it is cultivated and used to rule over and control people, however, we are crossing boundaries. And we have already crossed too many boundaries as it is. So, tell me... when, at which point, at which savings amount or bank balance sheet, can you switch from 'surviving' to 'sharing'? When will the 'naked fight for you existence' switch to the charitable attention for others? When?

Worldwide
Dominique Moïsi observed emotions culturally and worldwide. He states that the West (US, Europe) are being led by fear (especially for others and) for the loss of the national identity, the East (e.g. China) by hope and the Islamic world by humiliation. Muslims and Arabs have created a culture of hate because of a combination of spite from the past, restricted access to the world markets and religious conflicts (also through Muslims in the West). While the free West and the Muslim world prepare themselves to cross swords, a culture of hope, which focuses itself on a better future, exists in Asia. He concludes that the West must break through its fears, if it wants continue the race with the East. My own conclusion is that we should stop thinking in terms of racing and competition!

Complacency
The danger of our Western world is complacency. In all sections and levels of society. Someway we have all been put to sleep, drowsing off and chitchatting along, especially in this damp and moist little low country behind the dikes and up to 8 meters below sea level: The Netherlands. We are scared and 'in denial' when it comes to new (economic) challenges and would prefer to play the victim in our welfare state, soaked with pseudo-prosperity (… and as long as we can pump up and sell our gas supplies, we'll be alright).

We suppress the truth, deny the threats and learn to see things in perspectives because people are (apparently) equal, the world is waiting for The Return, and all others are bigger and thus have all the power (Calimero effect) and suffering is a part of life anyway. We rather donate some money and no longer (principally) energize ourselves to change wrongdoing or remain patriots.

As goody two shoes we hope for and literally buy appreciation, while the big European players tolerate us with a smile and maybe even lick their lips at the thought of getting near our saved and huge retirement funds (still up to 700 billion anno 2010 for a few million Dutch workers), which in thought they already have spent on their own goals or investment strategies.

The complexity of reality paralyzes us; the pace is too high, the expectations too great. Making the right and carefully weighed decision, has become impossible by the overwhelming affluence (of everything) and when we finally postulate our rancor, preferably loudly and anonymously as a desperate cry for recognition, attention, warmth, protection and appreciation.
And you? How about you in this respect? Which way do you go, where do you stand?

The modern questions of today and tomorrow are: 'what do you stand for, how do you keep yourself busy with what, what keeps you from sleeping and what are you afraid of? Where are the pitfalls and threats on your path, what makes you insecure, what worries you, what do you hold on to?' They are all relevant, individual questions amidst a, by now, unlimited and all-embracing world of chances, crisis's and threats.

> *I know you're out there. I know that you're afraid...*
> *you're afraid of change. I don't know the future.*
> *I didn't come here to tell you how this is going to end.*
> *I came here to tell you how it's going to begin.*
> *I'm going to show a world without rules and controls,*
> *without borders or boundaries. A world where anything*
> *is possible. Where we go from there is a choice I leave*
> *to you. (The Matrix movie)*

Believing and trusting

It is nice to watch great movies, read interesting books, listen to passionate speakers ... but it is even better to take a look at your own choices and preferences, motivations, convictions and assumptions and find out what really has value and offers real support (for someone else close by or for the whole planet), what you are authentic in and how you can apply that to your organization or fellow human beings. If need be, by repeating and embracing the authentic choices of others (like durability, people-planet-profit, fair trade, cradle-to-cradle, windmills, CO_2 levels ... etc), but preferably by relying on your own strength, love, care, beliefs, surroundings, situation, choices and by spending your own time and money and such. If you can't manage that with introspection, find an external foundation and starting point to rebuild (yourself) from. Want to be tipped where to possibly start?

> *Christianity is the companion of liberty in all its conflicts –*
> *the cradle of its infancy, and the divine source of its claims.*
> *(Alexis Detocqueville)*

Many have read, when searching Lucas 1 (NT), and now trust the foundation of their life to the only true and real Christ who said (John 14): 'I am the way, and the life and the truth'. Now either he is completely insane or speaking the truth. You decide.

I recommend him to you, so to find your personal freedom, the meaning and value of life and the lifestyle to match. And if you belief, know for sure and trust that He has liberated you, please do this authenticity check: are you're deepest motives more serviceable, embracing and relational by now? If so, welcome to the desert of the real!

Externally or internally driven

In a lot of Western countries we have been taught (by Christianity as well) that we should translate matters 'from the outside' to 'the inside'. Our own feeling might betray us; better accept the strict truth from The Bible. The values and rules of 'outside' are of greater value than what our soul, intuition or our conscience lets us feel, sense, and hunch or tell us (if we can even find out how to listen to it anyway). After the conditioning by our education and schools we have learned, above all, not to express our deepest desires and feelings all too conspicuously.

This can be quite a wise thing to accept, because uncontrolled internally driven behavior may hurt others and then we'll get worried whether that person (e.g. our child) will later 'fit' in the game of society and the working place, together with all the others. If we then later on in life finally and inevitably find our OWN way as more or less enlightened individuals (and involve our inner feelings, intuitive knowing, voice and unique point of view) we will, surprisingly enough often hit unfamiliar terrain.

> *If you limit your choices only to what seems possible*
> *or reasonable, you disconnect yourself from what you*
> *truly want, and all that is left is compromise. (Robert Fritz)*

Learning to express yourself is often surrounded with unfamiliarity, fear, insecurity, pain, sadness and surprise. Too bad, because our fellow human beings –especially the ones we love- can only enrich us if we show and let them know our inners beliefs and feeling by hearts. If we don't, what should they talk and react on then? Our new couch, which is designed by Jan des Bouvrie? The new BMW off-road or bigger house than the one the neighbors own? Your successes at work (to make your boss or the share holders richer)?

Or your next chance for a minor promotion in the corporate rat race? That is sometimes desirable small talk, sometimes even fun and sometimes delightfully thoughtless, but at the same time... it's totally unessential for becoming a human being, like the one you were made to be and have been created to be...

Strictly Personal
Authenticity on a personal level is showing recognizable behavior, which corresponds with - and is a logical translation from – your unique and strictly personal character as a human being. Part of which are your own 'point of view', your opinion, your unique attachment to numerous different things in life, your application of experiences, the expression of your emotions, being aware of your surroundings (including cosmic discovery and contacts, free energy, magnetism, 4D and 5D, bio and nanotechnology, pulsonics and particalization) and that of others. You have no idea; no clue what is known to a few at the approx. 30 levels above top secret.

Think and act based on, and in line with, your own convictions and faith and curiosity. Take nothing for granted as your aspiration becomes more and more focused on credibility, trust and reliability.
'Thinking and acting' authentically arises from internal reflection + the external realization of your purpose in this life and your value for others, stemming from your personal strength and your contribution to the whole. You can still be ridiculed, intimidated or discredited but it doesn't matter that much any more. You start to understand your purpose and are being able to (at least partly) realize it. For yourself, your employer, your children and other loved ones. Very related is the notion of spiritual growth, responsibility and accountability. Which in turn are related to a number of important and great values, such as: honesty,

comprehensibility, originality, reliability, consistency and integrity. These are the desired characteristics behind authenticity.

Rewards

The prospect of a turnover of authenticity is 'knowing for certain' and growing towards 'a solid inner trust'; it is one of unity and giving purpose; of making a promise and aspiring to keep it. Along the way 'suddenly' things, matters and events will strangely fit and coincide; you can see the synchronicity increase right before your eyes, as it were. Your charm and appeal increase (maybe even faster than you're oh so very important financial capital).

> *The reward for conformity is that everyone likes you, but yourself. (Rita Mae Brown)*

Being personally authentic also consists of the acceptation of your unpredictability, inconsistency and dark or shadow side. After all, if we express ourselves individually (no matter how), it is by definition a sign of authenticity and singularity. Every single thing in our existence, unfortunately, also has a flipside, a hurtful and dark side. Even the top level of authenticity you have reached, has dark qualities. That level is, by the way, not a matter of working towards the highest phase of enlightenment or something of the sort, to then become a guru or arrive at your mental destination.

No, it is a constantly effort, switching, fighting and adjusting your behavior and thoughts as a working and living being between other people of flesh and blood. Authenticity is not a matter of perfect continuous performance or some final mental destination, meant only for the select few, the power elite who are in possession of 'the knowledge', but rather an intention of living together responsibly, a wondering, conscious state of mind which makes you modest and stimulates you to relinquish your prior, egocentric life. It is a way of thinking, it inspires you to act and is also a motivation for the way you live, it can give direction to the daily routine of your work or the growth of others. It is (wanting) to hold on and to continuously learn to think, feel and act more authentically.

> *I'm convinced that being authentic brings a major benefit:*
> *you feel better being recognized for what you are ...*
> *an unique personality. That's rather a rewarding response.*
> *Isn't it? Now, how would that work out on a corporate*
> *level? It's the same! (Pleu)*

Alienation

Becoming conscious of your authentic you, might mean that what you are doing now is suddenly of less value. That makes sense, for the things you're doing came forth from other deliberations and intentions. So lay aside your 'old you' and embrace the new authentic you: sometimes more kind, often more patient, increasingly gentle, searching for the truth, speaking more clear, lying less and less, increasingly controlling words spoken, offering less and less opportunity to 'the dark side', wanting to act constructively, trying to understand the broad notion of 'love' as a word and action and trying to offer fulfillment for others, quicker to forgive, helping more often without pecuniary reward, trusting more on leadership from above than on that of people and practices daily in being content and above all ... grateful.

> *How does one become a butterfly?" she asked.*
> *You must want to fly so much that you are willing to give*
> *up being a caterpillar. (Unknown)*

It is an art for a leader to apply a new vision in the everyday reality, the world around us, and the organization (and also at home). A natural tendency towards isolation is fine for a little while, to come to your senses, but in the end, you won't be helping others. Prevent becoming alienated from yourself, but also from others (or the acquired assignment, job function or responsibility). Do what you have to do, but, from now on, do it just a bit more authentically. It is still required to make a good solid profit as a commercial company, and to make policies as a government institute, or to loan money and invest and to fire people and punish criminals based on the democratic set of laws and rules. Being authentic has nothing to do with being 'a wimp', but has everything to do with becoming ... more human.

Your own brand

Others will notice if you feel harmony, mentally as well as physically, and everything seems going well. If they do, you've nearly become a 'personal brand'. Especially when your behavior and opinion are built on core values and character, you are becoming increasingly valuable to others. You are recognizable, unique, complete, balanced and thus powerful. You'll start to notice this because you'll 'suddenly' attract people and attention and opportunities that fit you and have an influence on how others (are able to) live. You 'suddenly' own a unique selling point: yourself.

The things you subsequently are allowed to create make your life more pleasant and significant. Makes sense, for you now know where your strengths lie, what your own (strong) points are and based on which values you are able to make the difference for others. You have now created your own market and need. There is an immeasurable demand for more of 'you'. There truly is. When you follow your own inner passion and convictions and remain critically sober, no one can hit or stop you, only hinder you and slow you down.

Regard yourself the way large companies regard their brands or advertize themselves in the market as a 'personality'. And if you only have yourself to offer (as a small entrepreneur, for example), learn from the big brands, how they market, analyze and shape their brand, and apply it to yourself. Watch out for 'fakeness' though, and for greed and avarice, make-up behavior, 'window dressing', egocentric motives, etc. Keep working on yourself, by yourself. Choosing work forced upon you by others with egocentric motives, is no longer authentically productive.

> *Don't listen to "It's not done that way." Maybe it's not, but maybe you will. Don't listen to "You're taking too big a chance." Michelangelo would not have painted the Sistine chapel. Above all: don't listen when the little voice of fear inside says, "They're all smarter than you out there. They're more talented, they're taller, smarter, prettier, luckier and have connections...". If you follow a path that interests you, not to the exclusion of love, sensitivity and cooperation, but with the strength of conviction that you can move others by your own efforts. Do not make success or failure the criteria. The chances are you'll be a person worthy of your own respect. (Neil Simon)*

Nice job?

Michael C. Gilbert states that the word authenticity is originally a Greek word and refers to: origin and authorship. He observes that people reach a material and psychological deadlock when it comes to a feeling of community and the rigid hierarchy of power within old organizations. What really defines the authentic bond between organizations and employees is the commonly experienced purpose – and meaning - of the work they do.

A shared vision of how and on which we should work together, for a better world (more prosperity, happiness, ease, conservation, honesty and such) and a communal idea of how that would work in everyday life, will provide us with the mental room to get the very best out of people. People will then become creative and curious. We really want to be good at what we do and will want to become even better.

> What we really want to do is what we are really meant to do. When we do what we are meant to do, money comes to us, doors open for us, we feel useful, and the work we do feels like play to us. (Julia Cameron)

Appreciation and attention are nice rewards. We usually like to work together with others when we experience understanding, respect and a relation between them and us. We work harder, when our passion helps others along and we are at our best when that passion coincides with our singularity, talent and disposition. Even within an authentic working environment there will be conflicts, and especially in those environments, the space to look for win/win/win solutions is available; there is room to experiment and thus innovate on all levels (within the boundaries of money, time, use and necessity); there is some freedom with respect to how people want to work and where they want to work and the opportunity arises for an 'organic-ization' (organization being a cognitive, functional, rational and instrumental whole) to be experienced more as 'a community' (thus including factors as: emotional, affective, relational and emphatic).

To be
Facing the authentic people are those who suppress, limit, exploit belittle or alienate people from themselves. Life is, however, not entirely black or white.

Organizations and individuals are never suddenly 100% or 100% not authentic. It is a process of making (individual) choices and of external necessity. The point is to keep on looking and make a case for what is real, during which the search may be more important than the final goal 'to be' (a static 100%) authentic.

> *The beginning of thought is in disagreement,*
> *not only with others but also with ourselves. (Eric Hoffer)*

To be able to grow towards corporate authenticity, the authentic manager/CEO, who through 'touch', self study, therapy, reflection or for instance religious conversion has been personally changed, and the social public movement (for instance activism for the environment, anti globalization, climate), come together. A good place for these two to reinforce each other for the common good isn't the street, where the police will keep these two factions apart, but the working floor (and most of the work takes place in organizations, companies or institutes). If action groups force change, by causing damage or disgrace (e.g. no chicken meat from old school animal farms) and a supermarket feels itself forced to stop selling the meat out of intentions such as loss of profit or turnover, it still isn't an authentic organization with an ethical management, acting from an intrinsic conviction.

Tension

Are you familiar with the tension between who you are and what you do and what keeps you busy? Want to become happier with your job? Yes? Welcome the searching club of millions!
Change is knocking at the door. It's a change consisting of doing business with a positive mentality, and with a will to prove it is profitable to switch to authenticity as an organization. People will work with twice the energy, less absence, new enthusiasm and 'drive', opportunities instead of threats, inspiration based on

passion and determination through focus, friendship and perseverance, creativity, ingenuity and servant team spirit. Fear than has been replaced by a 'pleasant tension', asking for help and respectfully receiving and accepting it replaces uselessness, distant behavior, loneliness, incomprehension, boredom, macho invulnerability and elbowing behavior.

Once the fight is finally understood,
wonders are possible. (Mao)

This is possible in every conventional organization, no matter how big or small or in which sector it's active, develops its own character and this isn't exclusive for the 'alternative circuit' of loss bearing, heavily subsidized, unworldly new age hippies. If your directors still think it is, it's time for a firm reconsideration of your surroundings and the trends and developments, which are taking place all around the world. If you ignore that, you might not lose tomorrow's battle, but you will lose next year's war.

You and us
Servant authenticity gets the biggest chance within ... organizations. Through cooperation, for instance, authentic behavior derailing towards uncontrolled or emotional individual behavior is prevented. Being you is of course allowed, but setting boundaries on human expressions is and will always be needed and desirable. The two of you make more authentic individuals together, so to speak!
Comparing on your own behavior, emotions and impulses to those of others, is a grown-up expression of authenticity and prevents emotional damage to you and to others. Authenticity as a new wrapping for your old egocentric behavior or old autocratic management is, of course, not a step in the right direction (and nothing more than a repetition of the same steps, which made the change so desirable).

Sometimes you have to, and are allowed to take the lead within your organization in order to force a change, out of new inner conviction.

Have you, for instance, ever accepted a promotion without a raise? Have you ever helped bring about an unethical decision? Do you hear people within your company speak of humans as the most important 'asset', and subsequently redundancy round after redundancy round follows, while the work pressure increases, as do salaries ... of the higher level managers only? Do you have a boss who demonstrates, lives up to and shows the important values

within your organization? Someone who 'practices' what he 'preaches'?

As a CEO, make sure that the measures you take coincide with the message. When the mission and core values do not match the culture and actions ... it will feed the hypocrisy, the humiliation, the gap between management levels, the indifference, intolerance, rumors, resistances and opposition. When that translates into money, it will cost hundreds of thousands of Euros. Make no mistake; more authentic behavior really is profitable.

> *A wise woman who was traveling in the mountains found*
> *a precious stone in a stream. The next day she met another*
> *traveler who was hungry, and the wise woman opened her bag to*
> *share her food.*
> *The hungry traveler saw the precious stone and asked the woman*
> *to give it to him. She did so without hesitation.*
> *The traveler left, rejoicing in his good fortune. He knew the*
> *stone was worth enough to give him security for a lifetime.*
>
> *...*

But, a few days later, he came back to return the stone to the wise woman. "I've been thinking," he said. "I know how valuable this stone is, but I give it back in the hope that you can give me something even more precious.
Give me what you have within you that enabled you to give me this stone.

Authentic leadership fulfils the need for this positive leadership. By drawing from positive psychology, it tries to stimulate optimal self-esteem and psychological well-being. Authentic leaders will foster confidence, optimism, hope and resilience (Gardner, Avolio, Luthans, May, & Walumba, 2005). The most common used definition of authentic leadership is *"those who are deeply aware of how they think and behave and are perceived by others as being aware of their own and others' values/moral perspectives, knowledge, and strengths; aware of the context in which they operate; and who are confident, hopeful, optimistic resilient, and of high moral character" (Avolio, Luthans & Walumba, 2004)*. This definition is build around the assumption that with high levels of selfawareness, self-regulation, and positive modelling an authentic leader will be able to enhance the feeling of well-being of followers. They inspire the followers to be authentic themselves which will lead to the realization of a sustainable performance (Avolio & Gardner, 2005).

8.

Towards Corporate Authenticity

The most distinctive difference between conventional and authentic organizations is the common consensus regarding a mutual vision and regarding use & necessity of the reason for existence and regarding a positive goal.

Authentic organizations have a mission that appeals to customers, relations and suppliers, but with which people can also (more or less) identify themselves. Goals in those organizations often consist of a direct, tangible financial results as well as an indirect benefit for the surroundings, community or the social living environment. They do not simply work and exist for their own profit, but also for other people's profit.

Next to that, you can also recognize them because they are always mentioned as an example by opinion leaders and other authentic starters and seekers. You can recognize them as well, because people are always happy to join them or work for them, or because the employees indicate that they're very content and be able to contribute to the exciting goals and to a better quality of living together. Authentic organizations have no trouble looking for new people to hire, just because of their authenticity. There is your first benefit to be jealous of (and to save the high HRM costs), if you are not yet top notch authentic.

> *Classic economic theory, based as it is on an inadequate theory of human motivation, could be revolutionized by accepting the reality of higher human needs, including the impulse to self actualization and the love for the highest values. (Abraham Maslow)*

Basic principles

Consumers, customers, managers and employees are more often choosing individually and less predictably. Production is no longer bound to a single location and the origins of goods can't be traced back by the consumer anymore. All seems to be made in China or India. Products and services have become exchangeable. For companies (and governments) this means that, if they want to influence opinions – or even behavior- they have to become authentic first.

Value judgment and the willingness to buy are thus more and more dependent on the perceived quality and the vision and values of the sender, his or her DNA and the organization as a perceived entity.
The more credible these characteristics and the character of the organization are, the more people will choose in favor of this sender. If the credibility has been built from 'fake' identity characteristics, and has not been interiorized in some measure, it will turn against you. Only a well-founded presentation and communication that stems from singularity and authenticity is, from now on, credible and thus profitable. This requires systematic attention and existing

images, reputations and opinions must be taken into account when repositioning towards a more authentic company or institution.

Meaningful

The old-fashioned sales promotion or product advertisement to recommend a product or service is often completely detached from the sender identity (think of technical product innovations) or on the other hand completely relies on the credibility and reputation of the sender, company or government. Management, PR and communication agencies need to include both of these possibilities in their entitlements and in the tone of voice with employees and relations.

These agencies need to invest to understand the services; management drives as to succeed in viewing matters from the perspective of the organization. If they perform 'their standard trick' from an unworkable (mental) distance, like from a self-made creative of strategic black box, they will lose their own credibility. And that way we're back at where we started again: commitment reinforces credibility. People often chose my agency, PeterVanPeetzen, for they know I aim to really understand the client organization and the offer.

For everyone

The beauty of change is that a conventional organization doesn't have to start all over in order to become more authentic. An MT choice for authenticity, based on inner conviction or shared values, already is enough for a process of transformation within your own branch, sector or group. Still based on the current approach, culture, planning and offer. In the mid long term these will automatically evolve and be adjusted, there is no need to do that suddenly, right on the spot. Evolution takes place along the way, while working and producing, within the current company boundaries. After all, every new authentic person isn't instantly a wealthy guru or suddenly a successful guest speaker (or the contrary). For all, it is a process of discovering and repositioning together. It starts with the search for authenticity, where it is hidden, as it were. It begins with talking about what 'it' is really all about in your organization or institute. For whom you are, and what you contribute as a group. Sometimes it rather obvious and sometimes it's more abstract. But the chance of authenticity is always potentially present. Even if only because you, after reading this book, will be able to detect authentic colleagues quicker, those who already want to cooperate in another way and already are authentic up to a point.

> *If the only tool you have is a hammer,*
> *you tend to see every problem as a nail. (Maslow)*

After formulating the measures and steps for improvements (from 'ist' to 'soll') based on the adjusted core values, mission and vision it is then important to take another look at the product assortment and, if need be, adjust it. Then you will have really made a start. Intention = vision = energy = effort = result = happiness. You'll really be surprise at what is all suddenly happening, in yourself and for all the people around you. Serving a positive goal changes people towards being positive, constructive colleagues. It seems to be a miracle. Also, in the start destructive forces (also 'real' managers and employees) will have to be corrected. No omelet, without first breaking the eggs. Some will have to leave. Help them … reinforce them … in your, by now, authentic way.

Benefits

Successful, authentic organizations are capable of gathering a lot of attention and facilitate (offline and online) meetings while organizing these around their own theme and what they want to obtain through their products or services for a more real, sincere surrounding or world. They are also able to explain those goals very clearly and illustrate them entirely sensible, for they are entirely in their right.

That is the tangible turnover number two and this will reduce the marketing and promotion costs quite a bit. It just is cheaper being a receiving as well as sending telescopic magnet, which attract publicity and attention, than being a walled fortress, full of secrecy and with management hiding in an ivory tower.
Is there a chance within authentic organizations for the HRM costs to be reduced? For the absence rate to go down? For productivity to rise? As well as the innovative forces? You already know the answers, if you have read the earlier chapters. When people can recognize themselves in organizations with their own feelings of relevance and purpose, they will love to help and be inspired to become even more authentic together. The wheel starts spinning.

Some facts
Based on research in the Netherlands in the years 2004-2006, collected by personal branding guru and speaker Hubert Rampersad
- An organization consisting of 100 employees with 25% mental absence, will have a loss of at least 2,5 million euro's a year (NRC newspaper).
- 60% up and to 80% of all absences have nothing to do with illness, but rather with de-motivation, lack of pleasure and inner involvement (NRC).
- Employees indicate that 10 to 15% of their capacities remains unused (NRC). They spend a lot of time day dreaming, staring out the window, gossiping and chatting with colleagues, playing games on the internet, drinking coffee, fighting etc.

- The social costs made caused by psychological problems at work, are estimated at 4,7 billion euro's every year (Institute for work and stress).
- Insurance companies estimate the costs of absence because of stress at 3 to 6 billion euro's (PWNet)
- Badly functioning employees cost the Dutch economy about 7 billion a year (SHL).
- A manager spends, on average, about 30% of his time solving conflicts. TNO Arbeid calculated in 2004 that about sixty to a hundred thousand people call in sick because of a conflict every year.
- Two-thirds of all functioning problems can be related to an irate relation between employees. *About 10% of all wage costs can be traced back to this.*

From abroad
- 22 million active, unmotivated an impassionate employees in America (Gallup Poll, 2005).
- Gallups indicates that unhappy employees cost the American economy up to 350 billion USD by related labor productivity every year.
- The turnover per share are multiplied by 2,6 when employees are motivated and mentally committed.
- 70% of all American employees are not mentally committed to their jobs.
- 61% of the British labor force, 67% of the Japanese and a shocking 82% of the labor force of Singapore is not mentally committed.
- Unmotivated employees cost the economy of Singapore $4,9 billion; the working force is one of the most unmotivated in the world.
- 20% of all Australian employees are unmotivated, and they cost their economy about $31,5 billion dollars a year.

- Research amongst 1500 Australian employees indicates that 18% is committed to their job.
- In Europe the percentage of motivated employees is less than 20%.
- The motivation of the staff is highest in Brazil (31%) and in Mexico (40%). The lowest levels have been found in Asia.

Baloney?

Think along for a moment. About happy cooperation between colleagues without fear, contributing their time and energy on a voluntary basis to the common and hopeful vision (through setting goals, which cannot be realized on an individual basis). Dream with me about the leadership of servant directors who want to help increase happiness and peace of mind and who apply the instruments and methods, based on a sincere motivation to bind people together and let them all have a share of the profits.

> *You see things; and you say, "Why?" But I dream things that never were; and I say, "Why not? (Bernard Shaw)*

Please, do not go hallucinating or become all misty (the organizations is no commune and we've left the flower power hippies age far behind us), but inspire, talk, research, stimulate people to maintain their authenticity, guard, strengthen and search for the ultimate balance between cooperation and turnover. Based on effective motivation, in combination with being realistic about your business surroundings. Realism and soberness remain desirable, for even authentic companies may go bankrupt (or be bought, or encounter setbacks or have to get 'their hands dirty' because of redundancy rounds or reorganizations or wars). Remaining authentic in an unauthentic sector, is simply hard work with 80% sweat. However, Joe Pine and James Gilmore (authors) state: 'Our basic view is that authenticity is becoming the new consumer sensibility In other words, the buying criteria by which people choose who to buy from and what to buy. Increasingly, they don't want to buy the fake from the phony; they want the real from the genuine. The new business imperative, therefore, is to render one's offerings to be perceived as authentic by consumers.'

The other side

It is useful to already start a scouting expedition with the current board of directors (members approximately 45 or older?) in order to find out who and what is authentic within your organization. That search becomes urgent if you think of the profile of the employees who will become colleagues in the coming years. Generation Y is already partly active within your organizations. They are also called 'the echo boomers' and are born between 1976 and 1990. It's the generation that was raised with free Internet, YouTube and texting. They also find expressing and manifesting themselves, considering multiple options and accepting each other (even after the Dutch social 'depillerization' process and including the rights of women and homosexuals) very important.

They are even more individualistic than the generation of around 1960 and entirely used to online multitasking, gaming and having friends, who have to be kept up to date quickly and shortly. The extended mobile phone is a necessity of life. They're also called 'the cup kids', for if one of them was active in any kind of sport, they always were awarded a cup, just because they participated (no one was really allowed to lose, participation was more important than winning). They put pictures of their partner and children online, not on a classic mahogany desk anymore. They read the time by digital signals and they regard a wind up ticking clock on the wall as an exciting rarity. Their economic prospects are not without doubt. After Y2K, a growing unrest followed up the economic crisis and the realization that they would have to provide for the many elderly and ageing population, further on in their professional life.

Different mindset

They regard organizations as places where the fitting job should be adjusted to their life (to their character and interests) and not the other way around. Their self-development has to be regarded in relation to the society, through embedding in social connections and communities. This generation succeeds in mixing freedom with solidarity. Authenticity is – according to SMO2000- the all-embracing, crucial value.

> Authenticity is the ideal of the internet generation.
> In order to realize this, both components that shape identity, embedding and individualism, should have to be rewarded the place they deserve. Within an authentic person, both components have been integrated to a large extent (Van Steensel).

Furthermore they are often quite optimistic. The government and authorities have lost value according to them. New forms of idealism such as durability, 'green' and social involvement arises.
In the processes of making decisions, they focus on constant feedback and participation. Their maturity is postponed a bit; they live at home a while longer. They are direct in their communication and needs and less used to the 'subtle power play' and the 'political elbow hypocrisy' in their behavior, attitude and cooperation. Their parents were sometimes 'simply' let off and then begun for themselves as small entrepreneurs or as part timers. They're sensitive to deceit and are looking for emotional bonding with their work and employer, now that family ties and the old religious networks have evaporated. So, change your mindset and prepare, they will be your new fellow managers in a few years.

Generation Z

The following generation (born in between 1990 – 2005) is now, partly as teenagers, learning and 'absorbing'. They have access to nearly every means of online communication, media, platforms and gadgets. They are the first 'real' digital generation trained in the equality of men and women and the new forms of socializing together. Their interaction entirely takes place on the internet and the familiar, currently highly valued classic verbal and written abilities are becoming museum characteristic. Online, they are able to switch from direct action to feedback unbelievably fast and are searching impatiently for fast results, knowledge, satisfaction.

> *Each generation imagines itself to be more intelligent than the one that went before it, and wiser than the one that comes after it. (George Orwell)*

They take part in shaping society and digital cooperation, but are able to do so without the tight personal relationship or deep physical experience of real life meetings. Work is entirely in the extension of their primary talent and interests. Their interrelation skills and social tips & tricks are limited and a word like 'in company career' has limited added value. They will live their life, with their children later on (the Alpha Generation) in a virtual world.

Adjustments

The reputations, opinions and experiences of users with current organizations are shared on the internet quicker than ever and easily reach the millions of readers, users, followers and consumers within days. When you try, as an old school manager, to have control over the way opinions and images are shaped you are now entirely out of touch. Participating, explaining, coaching, illustrating, facilitating, stimulating and representing are your new functions.

A quick edit or fix or adjustment by use of only traditional media is only a small part of the efforts for some idea of damage control. Your new job is: willing to present authentically (content is depending on the reactions, appreciation and events that follow) and, in order to be able to do that: become authentic. Who is behind this event? Who supports this brand? What does that company stand for? What do they want to contribute anyway? Why do we allow them to exist? How can we hurt them in case of wrong?

> *If everything seems under control, you're just not going fast enough. (Mario Andretti)*

By means of the internet, monitoring all communications and actions and matching these with organizational principles and mission statements is quickly done. So, stop blowing steam, but give 'real-time' and accountable substance please! The current averagely and highly educated citizen clicks and switches quickly and is blatant and concludes 'logic'. If you promise A, and then do B, you're out as a provider (and you'll have no idea 'what hit you at the speed of light'). That goes for the consumer markets, business services sector but in the B-to-B environment as well. Gather round your colleagues tomorrow and subtly ask them for a shared company value or for a typical element in the joint culture. Heard any contradictions? Well, now you now know where to start.

The sender
Authentic identity management is … connecting your own unique spot with your motivation. Products are bought, because they have been made, assembled or offered by YOU. That aspect deserves promotion, a reputation and advertisement. In my personal contacts with managements, the best and most relevant solutions and options only arise when we are talking about motivations, the 'reason why' and the 'drive with which' they handle matters.

That is the base for a true authentic nomination of value and branding for that organization. The familiar list of superficial things: reliability, flexibility, quality really is a bit too meager and you must go twice as 'deep' to get to the bottom of the matter. The offer is subsequently 'loaded' with fitting emotions and targeted purpose. That will forge bonds and bring unity between the people internally as well as externally. The translation towards desired behavior of employees will then offer solid ground to stand on during the selection, remuneration and the just estimation of (in)effective characteristics.

> *Unless commitment is made, there are only promises and hopes; but no plans. (Peter F. Drucker)*

Consequently, do you employees, followers, participators or members recognize, believe, confirm and embrace what your organization promises in public? Has that ever been researched? Do employees think and live (more or less) in conformity with the corporate promises? Or is that still an inappropriate and strange expectation? To reach for higher levels of satisfaction, during changes or as a foundation for innovation, it is fruitful for those two to be combined. Synchronizing the corporate personality with the culture and the values is important for more consistency and trust. It's also important internally, to keep sharing, communicating and calibrating the promises and principles of existence to the conviction of your people.

Mental handles
- Redefine the reason for existence (why are we here?)
- Formulate the dream (for a better world, the moral compass, the vision/mission)
- Find out what 'acting ethically' means to you, your MT and your organization

- Balance motivations and passions as MT (for the benefit of all, between what you want to own/have and who you want to become)
- (Re)Define singularity (which offer, product is very related to our character or past)
- Secure the (positive) goals (remember: profit and ego are secondary)
- Define the value of money, turnover, profit (as necessity, but not as motivation; what do we do with investments in what)
- Describe the value of wanting 'more', what is 'better' and what is 'growth'
- (Re)define the core and the strength (unique skill, position, characteristic)
- Describe the added value of your organization (for your surrounding, the planet, people)
- Put organizational values to paper (around growth, cooperation and leadership, how to be the 'boss')
- Indicate what your responsibilities are and what you'll do as a leader (for the good of all, to get the best out of every individual)
- Make the influence of those involved tangible (the kind of subjects and the voting system, plus the ideal 'span of control')
- Secure the way traditional hierarchies and old reporting systems will be avoided (do not judge and monitor, but reflect and underpin, coach)
- Analyze where the fears lie in the corporate culture, canalize signals of stress and/or bottlenecks in processes and procedures, increase the pleasure (from presence up and to performance) and stimulate 'do after think'
- Also base your judgment on levels of motivation, commitment and passion

- Make choices about what you won't do and who you don't serve (principles first), aim for a more humanitarian organization
- Describe what 'selling' will be from now on (offer a platform, a start, measure, listen, understand reasons, complete things together, reward/share, deliver, guard, develop further, adjust and again: offer a platform, a start ... etc)
- Shape and build the community (offline and online) in the interest of all relations by meeting, moving along, listening
- Make it clear why you should deserve support (of users, clients)
- Indicate what motivation and ambition fits your organization (to do business with or to come and work for every day)
- Formulate a method to offer space for innovation and room for creativity (as a goal, not as a coincidental by-product) and pleasure
- Clearly and individually indicate where and how pleasure, respect, happiness and such must be regarded (for employees and suppliers, followers and clients)
- Design stimuli for behavior (reward integrity, honesty, keeping promises, and such and sanction negativity, destructiveness, egocentric behavior, power play)
- Measure the level of credibility, reputation and trust (internally, externally, of the management/MT/Board and of the entire organization and services, products)

Brands

Authentic organizations (eventually) have a brand or range of services that is strong, stands out, organic, relevant, meaningful and memorable. These brands fulfill an important functional and emotional role in the lives of clients or consumers and aren't quickly forgotten or, impulsively traded in. In the old economy it was all about marketing, packaging, image building, promotion and hard sales. Authentic brands should be 'accepted' (no longer 'sold' or 'pushed' with a lot of fuss, empty shells and 'launched' PR spin') because of their contribution, perspective, responsibility and underlying values. Based on which it was once started and for the passion and conviction with which it is communicated and sold while all understand the context in which it has added value.

That way, the new need for authenticity is satisfied and it will have contributed to a lasting reputation. That added value can be translated into a higher price setting. But the acceptation of that marketing trick is, again, entirely dependent on the investment which will be made (or won't be made) with that surplus profit. Authenticity affects all aspects of the way in which the company is run. Buyers know and feel like they are involved and appreciated based on human values (not because they have more or less money to spend). They buy beauty, purity, genuineness, moments of contact and recognize their individuality.

> *Finally, brothers, whatever is true, whatever is noble,*
> *whatever is right, whatever is pure, whatever is lovely,*
> *whatever is admirable-if anything is excellent*
> *or praiseworthy-think about such things. (Jesus)*

Brands represent a reputation and that means that users and clients have power over them, (by confirming their trust in the brand and the producers, or by spending time, knowledge, expertise or money in sharing their opinion and experience).

Qualities
Authentic Brands (AB's) and AO's (Authentic Organizations):
- Are focused on the community, with a clear passion and ambition

- Organizes its own meeting places (online or tea parties or coffee moments, think of Tupperware), which can be easily recognized
- Advertise their products less and organize more occasions for the public to see, feel, smell and experience and physically buy
- Show how they make 'it' or why they aim for which quality level, what responsible choices were made and how honest production methods were applied (a small mini book attached to every business shirt)
- Build a group of followers, without manipulation of opinions and feelings (which people will only accept from other group members)
- Are open minded to the thoughts and wishes of users (on the PC and email and networks and such)
- Are never truly finished, improvement will always be possible.
- Do not solely want to be used or bought for just earning more money (Linux, Open Source software)
- Are units that cherish their authenticity based on facilitating, coaching and consulting (eBay, Google)
- Are no longer busy with advertising overkill with forced effects and screaming messages, empty common grounds and commercial bombardments.
- Treat a client as a human being (instead of an infantile child) who has a free choice and regard customers not as a 'sales opportunity'.
- Want you to participate and think along in their core processes and do not use your slogan for free, because it saves them an expensive PR agency. If people participate, they e.g. get a % of the profit
- Also dare invest in so called less profitable services and smaller firms and institutions (Dutch Triodos and ASN Bank)

- Think along -with respect for privacy- based on behavior of their unique community of followers (Amazon advises and shows you what others have looked at, done and bought)
- Nurture and offer opportunities to speak and discuss with each other (many online forums)
- Realize that their followers, visitors and clients are the ones who 'load' the brand with value and keep the 'brand experience' alive
- Offer suggestions for research and show enthusiasm for everything that is pure and real (The Body Shop, Anita Roddick)
- Realize that the price, availability and quality are important, but that the user also has own feelings and individual emotions before he decides (Apple is experienced as innovative for people who think differently)
- Are in touch with green, animal, planet, wellbeing and worry about the future for children and the next generation

Grow

Gilmore and Pine confirm that a determining factor for success or failure is now whether your organization comes across as true, real, and not as a fake. They see two strategies (and advice the second one):

1. Aspire to reach full transparency, responsibility and visibility (be 100% clear in what you promise and say you are). The forerunners in term of behavior are often very strict and an almost sacred example. This creates expectations and the trust can disappear very quickly, when something negative happens (the bone in a vegetarian meal of a food manufacturer).

2. Act in perspective towards the outside world and above all, admit the point where you aren't 100% authentic yet and you, sensibly seen, cannot be yet. Communicate your vulnerability

and poke some fun at yourself if need be (and don't let others force you to this). Be honest about your plans and don't pretend to be better than you really are. Be authentic about your not being authentic, as it were.

In our experience society there is a need to discover what is sincere and what comes from inner beliefs, in between all the fake and forged emotions. Our reality is (far too) quantified, adjusted, edited, managed and has become far too commercial. Mammon rules and even Dutch queen Beatrix stated: the lie reigns. The future buyers and consumer are searching for what is personal, what resonances their interest, intuition and is lasting and memorable. That is what they're looking for, when it concerns successful authentic brands of the day after tomorrow.

Ready to

PR agency Edelman has drawn the following conclusion from their 'GoodPurpose' study 2009, in which 6000 people were questioned in 10 different countries:

- 61% has bought a brand that supported charity (even if it wasn't the cheapest brand)
- 57% rewards brands with their purchase if they have contributed to society
- 56% thinks social and business interests are evenly important in the decision process within organizations
- 64% recommends a brand that supports charity (12% more than in 2008)
- 75% would switch brands if the other brand (of the same quality) would support charity

Brands and corporate senders should have an interest in identifying a social goal and contributing to a charity project that suits them. Identification with an authentic, social goal is becoming important for customers. The study shows that 66% indicates that it's no longer enough for organizations to 'simply' give away money, but that they have to incorporate charity in their everyday affairs.

So that is clear then: doing well is an organizational attitude towards life and a real intention and only then: authentic in the eyes of others. This asks for a renewed purpose and mission statement for the brand policy as well as for the entire organization, if you have not adjusted them yet.

Charity

Protector & Gamble Co; speaks of the 'touching and improving theme', reports Advertising Age. Unilever top executive Paul Polman indicated that Unilever wants to come forward from behind their brands, to support their program Making Life Better (helping consumers look good, feel good and get more out of life). The question is, however, whether it's just a marketing trick, which just happens to correspond to the spirit of this century or it's an inner conviction that affects the entire organization. Only if the last is the case, the organization is credibly authentic.

> *Coming together is a beginning. Keeping together is progress. Working together is success. (Henry Ford)*

The start has been made; (change of) management culture and marketing are increasingly starting to be an extension of each other. Internal Branding rises from its ashes, as it were. They are the same things that motivate employees as well as clients and relations. Branding has become a form of experience, or even love and spirituality within authentic organizational cultures.

Employees are searching for the link between their individual convictions and value system and those of 'their' organizations. It is a quest for synchronicity of organizational with individual authenticity. After a successful link between the two, commitment and involvement follows. That is an appealing view, as past decades didn't exactly excel in embracing this way of thinking.

Unique singularity

Method (UK retailer in cleaning supplies) asks people during job interviews how they plan to keep Method 'weird and a little bit crazy' and practices a 'Humanifesto', which sounds like this:

- As people against dirty, we look at the world through bright-green colored glasses.
- We see ingredients that come from plants, not chemical plants.
- We're entranced by shiny objects like clean dinner plates, floors you could eat off of, Nobel peace prizes, and tasteful public sculptures. We're an e.o.m.e.d. (equal opportunity movement for environment and design). Method is our way of keeping the movement, well, moving.
- We're the kind of people who've figured out that once you clean up your home, a mess of other problems seem to disappear too.
- We always see the aroma pill as half full, and assume everyone we meet smells like fresh cut grass or a similar yummy, nothing-but-good fragrance.
- We think perfect is boring, and weirdliness is next to godliness.
- We believe in making products safe for every surface, especially earth's.
- We believe dirty, in all its slimy, smoggy, toxic, disgusting incarnations is public enemy number one, and good always prevails over stinky.

Trends

Agency Cone Inc. found out in 2009/2008 that more and more people wish to switch to a product, which is associated with charity

(79% now against 66% in 1993) and even 38% says they actually done so (compared to the 20% in 1993). Even though it is an American study, the trend is obvious.

I'm convinced this generates the cheapest form of marketing: positive (online) word of mouth advertisement, by employees and users, clients and consumers. General Mills' states: under the motto 'We Nourish Lives', employees test products and judge planned adverts. This way they contribute in extend to only performing their daily tasks in their daily routines. At the same time they have influence on the external messaging and quality perceptions. And that is a valuable characteristic of an authentic organizational culture.

SRE and durability

Socially Responsible Entrepreneurship (SRE) and Sustainability are hot. That is a positive development, towards a more authentic society and more careful use of resources and the environment. The purity of the motives and the reason behind measures are important factors for the credibility of SRE. Is it just a handy business opportunity to enhance profits? Are you 'simply' playing the trend, because you might receive EC subsidies or because everyone else is doing it as well? Is more money for your own selective group the issue? Are other interest served, behind the façade that is SRE? Is SRE forced upon your business by laws or regulations?

If motivations are forced or superficial, this is less authentic but also can lead to an improvement of living conditions (which already is huge progress anyway, authentic or not). Anyhow, SRE belongs to an authentic organization; there is no doubt about that. When the time is right, develop a deeper conviction along the way, so that in the end SRE is about the 'new essence' or 'new cooperation' towards a state of increased authentic coexistence between trend and belief.

Preferably, SRE comes about based on the conviction that more transparency is needed or as a sensible extension of the personal organizational values or the intrinsic conviction of the members of the board of directors. That way, authenticity is the 'trigger'. When that becomes visible for everyone, it will be a major leap forward for the happiness of everything living and for the credibility and the trust in the contribution of the organization involved. Those are the conditions for a new return and for a new attitude towards the definition of 'business results'. Studies have shown (Atos Origin 2007; website SRE) that the old-fashioned profit level can be at least 2% above branch average, when SRE comes in play.

SRE, sustainability and durability are valuable steps in the process of going from cold ego capitalism towards a full integration of business targets, human interests and the environment. From responsible entrepreneurship (SRE) towards durable commitment (SDC) to the, now introduced for the first time, final step of becoming: Durably Authentically Integrated (DAI)
Hopefully it'll be a matter of time and gradualness. DAI is my vision for our future and a necessary horizon when exploiting the next phase after this current economic 'credit based ego capitalistic debt model'.

It lives and it works
Companies having a proactive strategy in the area of sustainability, have a head start and a better chance of surviving coming uncertain market circumstances. Studies show, furthermore, that there is a positive relation between Corporate Social Performance and Corporate Financial Performance. Researchers Van Beurden and Gossling conclude in our Western civilization, that: 'Good Ethics is Good Business' Recording what that means exactly in 'Charters' and 'Codes' offering a framework for the way employees should act, is already taking

place. Asito cleaners is launching a 'Durable cleaning concept'; Sara Lee has made a 'Mirror Test' for its staff, Courier TPG is already one step ahead (from SRE entrepreneurship towards SDC commitment) through delivering logistic knowledge and free services for the World Food Program; the MSC hallmark for food is also valid within Unilever, Cradle to Cradle use of resources (German Miller, Trigeda shirts, KIVO foils); community involvement (Okura Hotels); Biofuels (Argos Grope, Solaroilsystems) and the many durable 'Purchase Conducts' at banks up and to beer brewers.

When you choose your SRE activities, please stay close to the core of your current skill, offer or existence. It is less effective and credible when smart researches are picking up the trash in the adjacent park while it is way more valuable if they e.g. research a new additive for less environment aggressive waste. Good SRE examples based on the singularity of a company are, for instance, TPG and Sun (dishwasher cubes) and supermarket chains with a more durable range of healthy goods.

Heart plus head

Let's go back to the start again: why do we want authenticity? What is the added value of 'soft values' as credibility and trust? The answer is simple: it makes us happier because we are able to grow towards who we, in essence, really are.

> *I don't know what your destiny will be, but one thing*
> *I do know: the only ones among you who will be*
> *really happy are those who have sought and*
> *found how to serve. (Albert Schweitzer)*

At the same time it is one of the most difficult questions to ask: Are you really happy? A lot more difficult than the obligatory courtesy phrase: is everything all right? We cannot assent to it for the full

100%, but we remember the true moments of happiness and the moments that 'everything was all right'. We experienced less fear and more hope. Posing this question on a corporate level is intriguing, but also highly unusual. It even makes people laugh: are you working at a happy organization? Even if we can't exactly point it out, the opposite is something we wish on absolutely no one.

Being happy

And when we are happy that really is a benefit and an important asset for success, right? Far more successful than operating in a corporate culture of 'are you all right'? Truly happy organizations, of course, do not exist. Only individuals in combination with authentic values, behavior and some basic principles for pleasant cooperation and appreciation can bring about and strengthen the collective happiness. For now, just make a goal out of happiness it, and subsequently measure its levels internally. I would be really very curious for the results!

A few characteristics of happy organizations:
- Communicate fun, vivacity and social character (and less serious and rational).
- Appeal to emotions (and afterwards to facts and numbers)
- Participate in the decision making process (being able to express your opinion more, being heard, being able to vote, and making various disciplines less isolated).
- Open and transparent exchange of information (less top-down, monitoring and less 'nonsense', everyone knows what the top wants and why decisions might deviate).
- Let the client, customer, member, constituents, sponsors, civilians and consumers in (spend less time on yourself and relate more to 'for who are we doing this and what do they want?')

- Have a stronger feeling of 'us' (you work AT ... and not FOR ..., in a team and on something essentially positive).
- Repeatedly express appreciation ('your contribution matters, we respect you, you make the difference and you are more to us than a Job Qualification summary'.)
- Give excellent service (always more, more polite, attentive, understanding, correct, compassionate than people expect. It may even cost money).
- Are open to ideas and adjustments (to really pioneer them and take them seriously)
- Cherish modesty (and a sense of adventure, silliness, passion, kindness and perseverance).
- Stimulate freedom wherever possible ('our dress code: you must wear cloths'- Google), with respect to working place, working times and reward packages.
- Practice pride sharing (of what you're doing together and are thankful for, plus what you are able to contribute).
- Play a game together (and learn to know the unique 'someone/person/ human being' and not the CV document, plus: stimulate physical exercise)

Personal Contributions

It's proof of a different 'state of mind' if you first look at what is going well and what may become stronger, instead of solving problems and put effort into what is going wrong (anyway). Cooperrider and Srivastava regard organizations as a miracle and a self-questioning unity, which appreciates what she CAN do and where opportunities can be found. They give attention to 'what is working' instead of fixing 'what isn't working'. This strengthens trust and provides space for a positive contribution of people. Based on the 'Appreciative Inquiry' you'll work better following 4 steps:

1. Discover 'the best of what already is' (where things are going perfectly in your organization)
2. Imagine 'what could be' (think of processes that will always work perfectly)
3. Design 'what should be' (what is needed exactly for those perfect processes).
4. Realize 'what will happen' (organize participation to realize it)

These are valuable steps if you intent to manage processes in a more authentic way. Next, I will provide a few additional ideas for happiness increasing intentions, which are related to your attitude and behavior.

Grateful

'Count your blessings' in a healing mantra and provides peace in a troubled (inner) world. If need be, make it a personal strategy and give it its own anniversary day (like in the USA). Entire nations do exactly the same. Anchor it in your culture, set the example yourself, make it your signature in all your emails, and let it be discussed or open meetings with it. Rest assured, there are plenty of those blessings, in your organization or in the vicinity, at relations or clients or even at your neighbors. Thank people for their contributions, their empathy, skills and their thoughtful behavior towards (sick up and to promoting) colleagues.

> *Gratitude is not only the greatest of virtues,*
> *but the parent of all the others. (Cicero)*

Thank customers, clients or your constituency. Be thankful in speeches and at meetings. Involve your followers or market and the competition as well (especially if they're doing better than you). If need be, make a top 5 every quarter and make it a returning subject in the intranet or your personal blog and find out what made people happy when they got involved with your organization. Whether it is material or immaterial, big or small, from a new assignment up and to a new staff dinner. Be amazed of all to be thankful for. Constantly think of new ways to stimulate gratitude. It will benefit you also.

Kind

Exercise and practice your kind attitude, way of speaking and deeds. To board members, relations or stakeholders as well as to other colleagues or suppliers. Also send those who are indirectly connected to the firm, e.g. a cake if there is something to celebrate. Appreciate the fact that they are your suppliers (and for once do not emphasize the fact, how much they've already cost you). Organize an open door day for the neighbors, arrange a breakfast for partners, and continue to celebrate 'Santa Claus' for the little ones. The positive effects, smiles, happiness, appreciation and gratitude will be substantial (except for that one whiner). It'll make you feel better as a manager (giving is simply 'good' for your ego too) and it strengthens the mutual bond. Someday it will come around.

Optimistic

This strategy is simple and effective. Always look on the bright side of life. Every coin has two sides, after all. Every bit of bad luck incorporates its bit of good luck as well. Let it become an attitude towards life and let it influence the annual reports, adverts and conferences. Never go along with the downward, negative spiral of bad news surrounding you, via your competitor or in the media.

> *Optimism is the faith that leads to achievement.*
> *Nothing can be done without hope and confidence.*
> *(Helen Keller)*

Always focus on what is good in 'us humans' and in your organizations and do not focus only, on what went wrong (completely ignoring it is, on the other hand, not a smart thing to do either). Just imagine where your organizations might be in roughly ten years. Imagine everything will go well on the road ahead. See people already working hard to accomplish that, together. Share the wishes, vision and perspectives in your (personal, written and corporate) communication, in- and external. Be amazed at the commitment of employees. Difficult? Follow a NLP course!

Accept

There is no business 'war' between competitors that have to be 'destroyed'. The market is no 'battlefield'. They are no 'barbarians' at the gate. It is no 'jungle out there'. Refuse 'vile and sneaky behavior' and bury that mental hatchet to 'kill kill kill' your competing board member and make new room for deep breathing and real progress. Come on! When you were a child you thought like a child and still drank your mothers' milk, now that you're grown up act like a man and eat solid food off your own plate (New Testament). So let that anger or frustrations go, write that woman or minister or CEO an imaginary letter (and whatever, NOT post it).

> *When I were a child, I spoke like a child, thought*
> *like a child and reasoned like a child, but when*
> *I became a grown-up, I abandoned everything I*
> *considered childish. (Apostle Paul, NT)*

Feelings of vengeance block any trust within your organization; consumes a lot of time in meetings and costs loads of negative counterproductive energy while a state of acceptance or forgiveness brings about new creativity, streamlines discussions and opens new ways for you to move on. Force people to deal with anger privately and just send frustrated, angry agitated people home (for the rest of the day).

Facilitate creativity
Successful companies and organizations constantly think of what is new and might also be useful. They appear to be in a state of permanent 'flow'. Find this flow and allow people to brainstorm and test ideas. Don't lock the building if people wish to continue working for a bit longer at night, install places where people can relax and introduce colors and create a pleasant working atmosphere in your building's interior and floor plan, also stimulate a measure of play, silliness and informality.
Appreciate the witty joke (even if it stings a little). Allow 'the boys to play together for a while' or 'to go against the current for a moment'. Don't instantly judge deviant behavior, rather question people. Curiosity is good, curiosity is essential. Appreciate the work people do for your organization in their own time, outside or even in their vacations. Ask their opinion about what they regard as 'the real world' and discover trends this way. Go outside more 'into the wide world' if you feel you need to, studying the competition for instance. Ask a group of students what they think of 'everything'. Always distrust people's reasons if they are based on: 'that's how we've always done it' or: 'that's what we're used to do'.

Invest in meeting
Personal interest is allowed again (till the level of sexual intimidation). Cold, haughty, formal and aloof behavior is passé. 'Management 'by walking around' and management 'by asking an open question' are back. Free up some time (which you are really able to do). Visit departments and show some interest, talk to people about their work and improvements and ask for feedback. Organize more brainstorm sessions and employ people at random (not always the same group).

Be correct, kind, mild and complimentary again. See the good in people, stimulate them.

> *The most important ingredient we put into any relationship is not what we say or what we do, but what we are. (Stephen R. Covey)*

Be available at important events (marriages, funerals, births, first day of work, exit moments, redundancy) and show yourself as a company as well as an executive. Finally send that personal note again. Put a real signature at the bottom of a congratulation card and throw all those stamps away. Do not make a distinction between people who are close by, or further removed from you. Reassure them of their strength and play along a while with 'their thing'.

Overregulation and tunnel vision

Too much energy is spent on that last 10%, on perfecting rules and support of even more regulations. In systems, processes and cooperation. Rules are needed, but often keep people small and a prisoner as well. Sometimes externals perform an audit to check the (e.g. ISO9000) rules, drafted by their own employees. Amidst all the fuss, people often forget that only those rules drafted by them can be checked, and this way they've actually built their own prison. Sometimes those rules or laws come from outside, and appointing more, more or more managers or staff often becomes the most sensible, but also the most impracticable result.

Making more police officers available on the city streets and more nurses besides the hospital beds are hot topics to be solved. Measures taken by governments and budget allocations only work partly. The energy and money is spent on more hierarchy, control, procedures and equipment and monitoring.

Personal insights from bystanders or experienced professional having an intuition or those with wisdom down the ladder aren't heard but 'silenced'. Taking a risk and listen to your gut feel or heart as decision maker, become unacceptable. Authentic organizations need fewer rules and fewer sanctions. People are more dedicated and committed and are more resistant and flexible during the hard times to come.

> *Don't be humble.*
> *You aren't that great. (Golda Meir)*

Not because more facilities have been made or new social plans have been agreed upon, but simply because they are involved and like their job and their company. Expensive AirFrance-KLM pilots will serve meals to passengers in hard economic times without moaning and are even thankful for the experience. Is something like that possible in your organization or is it tightly shut.

Celebrate the amazement

It's always the little things. We often only take note of only the big ones. Cherish the client who offers his observations, welcome the customer who is filing a complaint, and congratulate the employee who voluntarily picks up a piece of trash. Welcome the supplier who has a new idea for your cooperation. Enjoy the new art piece on the wall together, celebrate the turnover successes and take no customer for granted. Don't make standard access badge pictures with a white wall in the background (to save some money?), but consider those photo's a print of their character that embody the pride they have in their work and can be hung on the wall at home.

> *The only real journey of exploration does not consist*
> *of the searching of new landscapes, but of the receiving*
> *of new eyes. (Marcel Proust)*

Take notice of a blossoming flower, the scent of fresh bread on the table, the taste of real chocolate together with pure fair trade coffee. It makes (authentic) people happier. Conversation will become more relevant to all and will progress more openly. Reaffirm the pleasure to be with them and always thank them for their time and trouble. Look for those little mental photo opps and literally write blogs about your organizations and the experiences, people and adventures. Long live the CEO or top executive who doesn't accept an expensive large painting of himself when leaving, but gives away a book initiated by him when he leaves, about the people who cooperated in the years of his 'reign' (just an idea, you may also sponsor a new hospital wing).

Spiritual

In some strange way, a lot of people value a spiritual religious horizon that promises to someday reward them. It brings believers together and provides participators a more useful and sensible feeling. It holds value for them and through servant ship also for others. Strengthen and reaffirm the goals and values of the organization regularly, based on such a perspective. Go 'back to the basics' of life more often and research the 'need & necessity' of your existence, vision and mission. Stimulate reflection on results and actions and restore the value of thorough evaluation (this has often been ignored the last decades).

If need be, organize lectures and conferences on the meaning of an employed life and become enriched by the perspective of spiritual guru's. Invite employees to visit them, tell them about a certain book that shines on some new perspective; offer space for spiritual sessions or places of silence and peaceful meditation. Acknowledge the value of the spirituality and religious factors in company management. Remain clear, as an executive, about your background and choices, and neutral in your action. Aim for the wellbeing of all.

Stick to your trade
Consistency is important for a reliable reputation. The world wants you to be recognizable and accessible. How much organizations lose their soul, because their new CEO wants to make a clean sweep, is motivated to put a merge on his CV or want to adjust the companies' house style as a first signal that there is 'a new boss in town'? Sometimes it's necessary, but the motives are often not in the best interest of, or even comprehensible to stake holders. A small scale fits authentic organizations as well as appreciation for what once was.

People are happier when they can trace back the part they played and recognize their contribution. It might be weird, but happy employees are always working on a fun project. They don't just build a wall in a cathedral, but are helping to build a religious experience of thousands of believers. They don't just put a cap on a bottle of beer, but provide the possibility for a future drinker to relax. They don't work for the bonus arrangements of an unknown boss or scourge of the market, but rather work for more happiness for more people.

Present
You don't pursue happiness, create or demand it (please, do not overestimate yourself). It comes to you, if you are open enough, willing to accept it and susceptible to giving selflessly and irradiate attentive energy. Let the organization be known to its periphery and allow it to present itself. Don't hide but be open-minded to new developments. Use the new social media and blog, Twitter (or whatever will come next). That is something for (your) people to be proud of. People like to be reaffirmed of the fact that you're on course and let customers enjoy a stylish qualitative public appearance, through the use of attentive manifestations.

> *Presence is more than*
> *just being there. (Malcom Forbes)*

An authentic CEO does not walk around with flowers in his hair, but wears a contemporary gorgeous suit, if it fits the moment. Being unknown makes you unloved and: you don't need to shout to come across clearly. Appreciate correct manners and share the desire for them. Authentic leaders don't have to wear overalls or dungarees. You know how perceptions work, how imago comes into being, but you never abuse that knowledge.

Four main characteristics of authentic leaders: 1. not fake their leadership, they are true to themselves. 2. from conviction they promote a value-based cause, as an alternative to status or honor. 3. Authentic leaders are originals, not copies; 4. Their actions and talk are consistent with what they believe (Shamir & Eilam, 2005). Without a moral component of authentic leadership, the construct is not of use. One could say that, to a certain extent, leaders such as Hitler, Stalin, Pol Pot, and Milosevic were authentic. They were 'true to themselves', they acted to their true beliefs and values, although their leadership methods cannot be regarded as authentic leadership. However, they lacked the moral capacity to serve in an ethical manner, leading to unimaginable cruelties. The moral capacity of the leader will decide on whether the leader will recognize a moral issue (J.H.M. Gerrits leadership 2009). What new 'manager of tomorrow' are we looking for? Who can live up to the demand? Who will be the one that will make more people happy?

> *Now we see things imperfectly, like puzzling reflections*
> *in a mirror, but then we will see everything with*
> *perfect clarity. All that I know now is partial and*
> *incomplete, but then I will know everything completely,*
> *just as God now knows me completely (Aposte Paul, NT).*

9.

The New Manager

A new generation of top managers has emerged. They value customers more than shareholders again. Short-term goals are followed by long-term strategies again and most of all, backed by vision. Options are opportunities again (and not a future deal to plunder and pillage). The new CEO's motivation is based on his inner values.

There will be a change in the way people think, in terms of service, market, product and assortment towards a more ethical determination of value, of services and products and of social responsibility. CEO's are involved with 'their' people and the offer again and aren't just there to make a lot of money real fast. Ego capitalism will definitely have capitulated in between the years 2013 – 2019. Top executives at large companies will be trusted by their employees again and will enjoy renewed social status.

Vision
The old command-and-follow-me method has been replaced by a model of cooperation and a more facilitating way of being in charge (especially in The Netherlands). Top down hierarchies are getting

less and less popular and are slowly but surely being taken down to make space for initiative and innovation. Knowledge is widely available and, for a longtime already, not solely the domain of the top anymore. Younger people really won't work five to ten years and remain all docile and wait for the next step in their career at the same company anymore. High potentials and other promising employees do not work for more status or money anymore.

People are most of all looking for personal satisfaction. As a talented human being or professional, we want to be of significance for the organization and the sphere of influence around it. In the fifties, sixties and seventies, you'd just work as hard and as long as possible ('hey, who is that man who cuts the meat at dinner every Sunday?') and for as much money as possible. No one ever asked if your job was 'soul satisfying or fun', above all work was 'useful'. One would look for 'fun' outside working hours. After that, the generation who wanted to become, and needed to find 'themselves' came along. They went for jobs that 'befitted' their talents, character, predisposition and interest. Working conditions had to be in balance with their private circumstances, like raising children together, marrying career woman and, if need be, part time or via job sharing. The first modern men succeeded to let (their) women take the lead. Slowly women are also taking up the coveted positions at the top, based on their intrinsic 'womanhood' (and not because they are good at imitating, or acting like, men)

> *You have to leave the city of your comfort and go into the wilderness of your intuition. What you'll discover will be wonderful. What you'll discover is yourself.*
> *(Alan Alda)*

From the heart
The coming years we will need leaders who are able to represent

organizations through the use of shared values, while also binding people to these, from their hearts (and, of course, their mind). They inspire trust and credibility with all stakeholders, as well as with humanity as a whole. It is a quest for something bigger than your own interest and concern. You can't realize that anymore, with more regulations and manuals, training programs and solvency or compliance systems. Because these only require even more attention and consume time, for they have been forced upon people and people reject them. But most of all because they're limited rational 'matters of the mind and not 'matters of the heart'. It's an essential balancing act to combine the two.

The new CEO has a personal integrity level of about 99,81%, she communicates openly, shows herself, delegates less if it concerns the corporate culture, HRM and representation and is working to promote inspiring and strengthened authentic leadership within the organization.

Personal goals are subordinate to general goals. Reports aren't just about the numerically targets like changes in the - or + or the % (those are daily visible on the IT management info dashboard) but about the qualitative experience, ethical principles and about what inspired people and about the 'happiness factor' in mutual relations.

Doing the right thing

People can be motivated with their contribution for 'quality', with a tangible added value as an organization compared to competitors and by enhancing service levels for customers (and not primary, through a higher stock value on the stock exchange). The new CEO's succeed in bringing back the human scale in combination with a serviceable, cooperative, worldwide umbrella of intercultural collaboration of equals, colleagues, clients, suppliers and self employed super specialists.

How wonderful it is that nobody needs to wait a single moment before starting to improve the world. (Anne Frank)

Leaders can be addressed on their consciousness and asked whether they have done 'the right thing' for e.g. their followers or country. Internal tribalism, arrogance, political intrigues and 'us versus them' will be eliminated in organizations. Promises are kept and from now on people will apologize when they were wrong. Based on the made mistakes, they will actively look for apt compensation for those who experienced any trouble or damage, because of those mistakes. Some day soon, if you show destructive behavior, mislead people or act in-authentically, you will be fired.

Characteristics

Gary Hamel already wrote down some new focal points for managers (Harvard Business Review 2009). I recognize a lot of what I sense is proof of authentic leadership tomorrow. If you as leader want a sensible set of measures and action, please read carefully what he has written down and reflect where you stand today. Points chosen, from his articles about Management 2.0:

1. Make sure that all the management's work serves a higher purpose (work for noble, socially significant goals)
2. Embrace and embed ideas of community and citizenship in management systems (practices and processes reflect the interdependence of all stakeholders groups)
3. Strengthen management philosophies with philosophical foundations (based on biology, theology and e.g. concepts as the new democratic markets)
4. Eliminate the pathologies of formal hierarchy (give informality a chance, leaders will step forward by themselves)
5. Reduce fear and increase trust (distrust is toxic and very destructive to engagement and innovation)

6. Redefine leadership (people are through with the heroic decision makers, leaders should be social system architects who facilitate collaboration and innovation)
7. Expand and exploit diversity (value variation, disagreement and divergence as much as conformity, consensus and cohesion)
8. Structure and aggregate smaller entities (become more adaptable, creative and agile than the large, slow organization colossuses)
9. Reduce the pull of the past (we often just copy past systems that obstruct change and innovation and only reinforce the status quo)
10. Define the common course more democratically (everyone has a vote based on commitment and share of voice is a function of insight, not power)
11. Change the reward systems (reward based on reaching short as well as long term goals, using holistic performance measures)
12. Empower the scope of employee autonomy (support grassroots initiatives, local experimentation)
13. Depoliticize decision making (undo these processes of positional bias and power play and make use of the insights and collective wisdom of everyone, give creativity what it needs)
14. Enable group formation based on shared passions (to stimulate as much commitment as possible)
15. Retrain managerial minds, humanize the language, value timeless human ideas such as beauty, justice and community as much as the traditional business targets like efficiency, competitive advantage and profitability and such, unleash human imagination, create internal markets for ideas, talent and local experimentation.

Motivate to affect

The top executive of tomorrow allows himself to be guided by principles and moral and servant values. Supervision and dialogue around character building, intuition, an authentic atmosphere and motivations are a part of any future MD program. Promote people answering: how does he control the way people think and act? Who or what determines her motivation? What did they learn themselves? Where lie my own triggers, beneath the surface of rationality, where I dare not look yet? What insights and wisdoms were breakthroughs in the way I think or feel? Which emotions did I conquer in the process? Trust (in yourself and others, from the inside and the outside), integrity and 'walk the talk' will become essential characteristics of a new 3O leadership, consisting of an 'Open Mind, Open Heart and Open Will' (Scharner, Jadernoa and Hiyashi).

> *The trouble with having an open mind, of course, is that people will insist on coming along and trying to put things in it. (Terry Pratchett)*

People are waiting for a leader, who is involved, sincere, wants to be clear and who is authentically 'genuine', who knows how to move and affect people, who can be personal and can tell the story that binds together. These leaders are able to find the balance between their mind, logic and ratio and their heart, intuition and emotion. They by nature keep the initiative and, of course, still plan ahead for the good of all. They read the future and foresee events based on arguments and are thus able to make the right choices in all (unexpected) circumstances. They provide a clear framework, feeling of safety and control (e.g.: by 'charisma controlled systems') and recognize deviation, rebellion or opposition by 'checks and balances' on the core values of the organization.

Rules for everyone

Acting predictable and being consistent are important characteristics for trust. Rules apply to everyone and especially to you. When you ask your people to work overtime, you'll stay as well. When a sale or acquisition is important, you will also visit the prospect. When budget cuts are necessary, you will be the first to discard the board limo and start driving a Toyota Aygo. Your staff may address you on all the values and principles that also apply to them. Your remuneration packages are understandable, sensible, accepted by a majority and entirely transparent.

All employees and middle managers watch 'the boss', simple as that. It's been that way for decades and it will never change. That means you have the responsibility to be the first to do good. You can't stay out of sight and let the staff suffer because of your pleasure, relaxation, role and decisions (because your are the one to solve the problems or are responsible for the right measures). Policies and practices coincide with mission and assortments, the umbrella vision and with the behavior of people (higher or lower placed). That is a principle matter of agreed upon authenticity, loyal to letter and spirit.

Appreciate and praise

We all either lack appreciation and recognition (Generation X), or find those two completely self-evident (Generation Y). Still, these two are the basic tools of the authentic manager and cannot be handed out enough to both generations (and all others as well). How we crave, as humanity, to be acknowledged for whom we are and how easy it is to make us gloat of pride and to motivate us to step up a little.

The CEO's of tomorrow is full of apt appreciation and subtly praises everyone's effort and contribution, either personally or publicly. It's positive, always comes around and forges a bond (and not an obligation, like we often think it does).

> *Appreciation is a wonderful thing: It makes what is excellent in others belong to us as well. (Voltaire)*

The same holds true for customers and suppliers. Also for them it stimulates and is easy to bring into practice, at least after you've removed the barricades, by thorough reflection, which incite you to only make calculated, even miserly expressions of appreciation or praise. It will benefit your people, their behavior and the general atmosphere. And accept that colleagues won't automatically expect a tangible reward or an upcoming promotion, they really won't.

Some behavioral tips that might sound simple but are very hard to apply in practice:

1. Thank someone personally (or by email, a written note). It really does count and it will make him feel less anonymous.
2. Listen, ask more questions and afterwards come up with an answer. People will feel like they are heard and are taken seriously.
3. Emphasize the positive. Always start by telling people what you thought was good or right. This opening will pave the road towards acceptance of that which follows. There is always something positive to be said first.
4. Inquire how you might be of assistance. Ask it because you mean it, not out of common courtesy. Be open to the answer and value it. Provide the promised follow-up.
5. Act natural. Talk and communication based on the language of your heart and conviction, interests, passions and values. Illustrate them if need be. It creates an open atmosphere and approachable attitude.
6. Keep going. When you once notice it does work ... from your smile to a rise in output productivity ... keep going.
It is never enough. Watch out for exaggeration and overkill

towards one single person.
7. Plan it in advance. Actively look out for that aspect or issue, which could be subject of your thanks or praise today. It strengthens relations and is never unwanted.

Offer people the space for them to get used to it and subsequently, don't make fun of any shy or timid answers, out of insecurity about 'what the heck is suddenly happening to them'. Enjoy your own exemplary behavior being copied by others (and be watchful in case they overdo it). New leaders don't necessarily have to be in the centre of all attention. Subtly and wisely they push their employees in the spotlights (not because of strategic tactical, but of authentic reasons) and let them get all the credit.

New leaders are functional, nuanced and embrace duality instead of underscoring it. Their relative modesty also makes them more vulnerable (but that is appreciated even more so).

Turn inwards

Paul de Koning regards personal growth and company management in relation to his 3A-model. It is also based on his inner conviction that there is another way to look at the organization and to ourselves. Analyzing and identifying, first requires a 3-step study inwards.

1. *Aspiration and ambition.*
   What is our aspiration, our deepest, inspiring wish, what do we stand for? When it becomes known we shall also have the ambition to realize that wish: we go for what we stand for.
2. *Aptitude and affinity.*
   In our authentic desire lies our aptitude. We have affinity for that one thing, which we also have talent for; then we can rely on ourselves being able to succeed with it.

3. *Attention and alertness.*
   We go to work now, with full attention, alert for delivering added value brought about by communal activity and on the look out for (unexpected) coincidence, meaningful turn of events. We are alert to synergy and synchronicity.

   Synchronicity reveals the meaningful connections between the subjective and objective world. (Carl G. Jung)

Hubert Rampersad summarizes growth and Personal Branding in four phases:
1. Authentic 'Personal Branding'. Concerns defining, formulating, applying and cultivating your personal authentic ambitions, your 'brand' and your characteristics.
2. Adjustments to your personality. Your personal brand reflects your true self and is familiar with a moral code of good conduct, based on your ambitions. Then it will become visible who you really are, what you really want and what affects you and your passions. Your authentic actions and behavior inspire trust.
3. Authentic 'Corporate Branding'. Defining, formulating, applying and cultivating the corporate ambition, brand and characteristics.
4. Alignment to the organization. Adjusting and synchronizing of the personal with the corporate brand. This results in more involvement, a pleasant, challenging environment and happier employees.

He pleads for distinctive behavior based on integrity, with vision, wanting to serve, modest, egoless and spiritual and with self-knowledge. Self-knowledge and ego must be balanced in order to develop personal charisma, trust and acting ethically. Leaders thus create credibility with a positive effect on the involvement, motivation and effort of their followers or employees.

Speak authentic
Language is the vehicle of the mind. We often have to do our best to perform 'right' in front of groups. Natural behavior and performance is the objective. Two things are important to be able to speak authentically:

1. Dare to allow and experience silence.
2. Eye contact with one person at a time.

Now rediscover how people 'really' listen to each other or to you. It doesn't matter whether it's a presentation or a meeting. In all situations it is eventually about the relation you start with the other, no matter how short. Give attention and you shall receive it. You're presence alone is already inspiring. Want to speak more authentically? Learn to apply the following: distance becomes connection; performance becomes being present; waiting for becomes listening; speaking to becomes speaking with; tension becomes ease; acting become authentic, true behavior.

> *We cannot let another person into our hearts or minds unless we empty ourselves. We can truly listen to him or truly hear her only out of emptiness. (M Scott Peck)*

Moral leadership
Moral leadership departs from pure, servant motives. Choices are partly made based on rational deliberations (this we already know), wisdom (what we sometimes notice) and partly based on motives such as selflessness, compassion or fairness. These last three are all quite subjective and stem from feeling, character, conscience, intuition or 'the voice of our heart'. It sometimes makes decisions hard to follow (or: logically retraceable via a conventional

costs/benefits model as only guide) for those who relatively are 'outsiders' to our organization. It requires first an exploration of the deeper values and management style of the organization.

Popularity, fame, honor, greatness and wealth are no longer the driving forces behind a moral leader. Leader do wonder, however, whether they can justify their decision based on the core values, ethics, what is good for others, respect for human beings and the surroundings and (thus?) based on a clear conscience. Moral leaders do not always choose the highest turnover in terms of money or shareholder value, but, don't destroy these returns either. Profit and growth are means to an end, not an end in itself.

> *The fact that man knows right from wrong*
> *proves his intellectual superiority to other creatures;*
> *but the fact that he can do wrong proves his moral*
> *inferiority to any creature that cannot. (Mark Twain)*

Servant leadership

A servant leader isn't a soft leftie and will 'do what needs to be done' in the interest of the company and all the people working with that company. A wise experienced servant leader is often a well-balanced personality. His actions are not 'ego driven' but serve a greater purpose. Robert Greenleaf drafted the characteristics of The Servant Leader:

- *Listening (actively and involved).* Leaders show their qualities for an important part in the way they communicate and making decisions. They want to know and understand the real intentions of a person or group. They want to be open to what is said and (especially) to what is not said.
- *Empathy (which leads to understanding).* They strive to understand others in an emphatic, sensitive way. They reason trusting good intentions and do not renounce them, even if they are forced to adjust their behavior or performance.

- *Healing (regarding a group as well as an individual).* A lot of people are not balanced as a personality and have contracted a range of emotional injuries, which is a part of being human. Leaders recognize an opportunity to help others 'heal' a bit and to live in harmony.
- *Awareness (self aware and in general).* Consciousness in general and being conscious of one self makes the servant leader stronger. Greenleaf noted: 'consciousness provides no peace of mind or encouragement. It disturbs the peace and awakens'. Good leaders generally are people who are 'on edge' and 'disturbed' in a reasonable manner. They do not seek peace of mind. They have their own inner calm.
- *Persuasion (showing the way).* Another characteristic of servant leaders is to practice 'explaining and convincing' instead of relying on authority. They seek dialogue, unlike debate, which often provides only one winner, and many losers. A servant leader knows that consensus and commitment are required to bring vision and mission into practice.

> *Those whom you serve, will grow as a person, will become*
> *More self conscious, wise, free, independent and will develop*
> *Themselves in such a way, so that they will also want to*
> *become more servient (R. Greenleaf)*

- *Conceptual thinking.* They have the ability to 'dream great dreams' and develop a vision. They think beyond today's reality. They are able to make employees enthusiastic in a very catching way for their mission, whilst not losing their sense of reality. This makes them highly effective.
- *Foresight.* Anticipation enables the servant leader to understand the lessons of the past, the reality of the present and the probable consequences of a decision in the future. Anticipation is deeply ingrained in intuition. Some are born with it; others

develop it while leading.
- *Stewardship (care for what has been entrusted to them).* The management, board of directors, staff and employees all play their own vital role for the preservation of the organization in the favor of the greater good of their society.
- *Commitment to the growth of people.* Servant leaders go out of their way to get the best out of individuals. They believe in the intrinsic value of people, which is more than factual output. Hence they are involved with personal and organizational growth.
- *Building community.* What is needed to rebuild the sense of 'community' as a viable design for more happiness? Servant leaders point us in the right direction; not by elaborate actions, but by showing their own unlimited liability for a specific community.

Effects

Inge Nuijten has, in three studies, determined what effects servant leadership has on its employees, teams and organization. The results are summarized in her thesis 'Servant Leadership' and indicate that servant leaders are associated with successful institutions. Servant leadership has a positive influence on its employees' wellbeing, team performances and trust.

The study also shows that servant leadership provides three important basic psychological needs of employees: autonomy, being connected and competence. This form of leadership also has a positive effect on team performance. Lastly it indicates that servant leadership is positively correlated to trust.

Serving is universal

The personal satisfaction as consequence of serving others is acknowledged globally. To serve others is a fundamental, universal human value.

It is emphasized in the teachings of the great global religions as well as in the statements of many respected thinkers and leaders. Kent M. Keith gathered a number of examples: the classic Taoist text, the Tao Te Ching, states that the 'way of heaven is to do good onto others and not to harm them'. The Buddhist text, the Shantideva or Guide for the Way of the Bodhisattva, tells us: 'if I use others for my own purposes, I will also experience slavery myself. But if I give myself for the case of others, I will experience nothing but stateliness'.

When it comes to great thinkers let us quote Aristotle, who said: 'What is the essence of life? To serve others and do good'. Cicero, the great roman orator and philosopher, said: 'People have been brought to life in the interest of other people, so that they can be good to each other'. Martin Luther King Jr. said: 'The most lasting and important question in life is: what are you doing for others?' Rabindranath Tagore, the Nobel Prize winning Indian poet, said: 'I awoke and beheld, life was service. I acted and behold, serving was joy'.

The Bible (Philippians 2:1-8) shows us that loving is serving one another and willingness to sacrifice. We have to experience the same feelings of Love as Jesus in our hearts. Only then will you become a servant, like Jesus humbled himself taking the very nature of a servant. Then you will renounce your ego and your own interests and will you serve the interest of someone else. Then you will practice Love. Jesus did not come to be served, he came to serve and offer his soul as a ransom for many (Matthew 20:28).

Male or female

Both are able to be the new, authentic leaders. Naturally. We are seeing more and more 'feminine men' (that doesn't mean unmanly) and more and more 'feminine women' (Tomboy models are passé) at the top. Femininity is persisting. It starts at primary school. How many boys get a male tutor still? The past decades, men especially occupied the largest number of top corp. positions, and we all know how that worked out. Characteristics like compassion, honesty, creativity and empathy, qualities attributed to women more, are a welcome addition to the male strengths such as decisiveness, straight forwardness, networking and strength.

Women have innate social skills such as team spirit and a dislike towards domination and subjection. There are more content driven and motivated according to Helen Fisher and being authentic to them means, first and foremost, to be able to be a good people person. Men only see the competition (I am the best and strongest) and successes are their conquests. Women have the overview, are integer and translate their success more into benefit or happiness for everyone. Being an authentic leader is cut out for both sexes. Sensible modern males possess a lot of the qualities attributed to women and vice versa.

New classification
Men are now able to empathize just fine, really aren't all ADHD autistic (and so what), and are caring and willing to express their emotions without problems. This makes them stronger, more genuine and thus, more authentic. These qualities are not by definition acquired at the expense of the male courage or thoroughness. Women are able to make decisions just fine as well, just as they also dare to be strict and clear if it serves the interest of the business or rather, the interests of the people. Their bitchiness is often exaggerated (especially if they reached the corporate top) and they succeed in wrapping 'it, the message' a bit nicer.

> *So God created man in his own image, in the image*
> *of God He created him; male and female*
> *He created them. (Genesis)*

Their political instincts are getting better, their 'power game play' ability is growing and both men and women can handle tough cases, crack problems and solve conflicts. Being able to complement or amplify each other in an MT or council or board of Directors (or in meeting and even clerical leadership) insures a good balance with respect to maintaining relations, ability to learn and develop, controlling changes, motivating people or achieving results and increasing the turnover with the whole team.

Intuition

While you take authentic risks, logic, facts, intuition plus feeling are working together quite well. The use of the last two isn't vague or woolly anymore. Everyone is familiar with it: you can be convinced in a meeting by (seemingly) rational arguments while, at the same time, you have a gut feeling (= knowing) something wasn't right. After a few times you will learn to listen to this 'inner sensor' better. Opinions based on your gut feeling have a negative reputation. It is regarded as some kind of primal reaction from the lower, uneducated, unenlightened class. This is entirely unjustified. Knowledge did not bring us any feeling. Intuition isn't an obvious result from knowing. You know 'something' without being able to logically explain it, without being able to provide any sensible rational explanation.

Tool

New top managers must have lots of intuition. Intuition is your private frame of reference of your knowledge and experience and life wisdom. Intuition often consists of experience. Someone who has worked in one branch for a long enough time has developed 'professional intuition'. This is difficult to share, communicate to e.g. students or to give away. It keeps you alert and warns you of something that can or must be done differently. In an authentic environment a decision based on intuition will be taken seriously, after which a process of analyzing and value determination will take place. In a conventional environment it will never go any further than stating 'it doesn't feel right'. By the way, the manager who repeated that phrase three times in a meeting was undoubtedly told to leave eventually.

> *All great men are gifted with intuition. They know without reasoning or analysis, what they need to know.*
> *(Alexis Carrel)*

Built-in consultant
Intuition may be discovered and unveiled by just going 'inside' for a while and 'listen' to your gut, physical or conscience's reaction. When someone has this at his disposal, he should learn to use it. It is valuable knowledge, but this time not coming from the brains. A credible leader succeeds in making his intuition intelligible. It's actually some sort of built-in consultant.

Besides, the presumption is that females have intuition at their disposal, and males do not (by nature). If intuition is a 'yet unclear form of knowing', men and women will be able to develop 'a clearer picture' of the situation at hand, dependant on how long they are working in a single branch. One difference might be that women tend to listen to it sooner. Authentic men dare to make better use of their intuition, learn to regard it as something normal and dare to take action based upon it.

With love?
The height of servant leadership is taking action –or marketing the new product – based on the motive 'love for one another' or 'for something that is greater than us'. Only then will the manager be truly in conformity with the famous trifecta 'faith, hope and love, and the most valuable of the three is love' (for your profession, your fellow man). Love is a tempting subject to delve

even further into, but we mustn't become too abstract. Is giving love (not the sexual one) a taboo in organizations or is it the ultimate form of authenticity?

Corporate authenticity is clearly related to the measure of how lovingly and selflessly you give and share to and with others.

> *We encounter spiritual issues every time we wonder*
> *where the universe comes from, why we are here,*
> *or what happens when we die. We also become spiritual*
> *when we become moved by values such as beauty,*
> *love, or creativity that seem to reveal a meaning or*
> *power beyond our visible world. An idea or practice is*
> *"spiritual" when it reveals our personal desire to establish a*
> *felt-relationship with the deepest meanings or powers*
> *governing life. (Robert C Fuller)*

Sensitive

'Love' is still a taboo word in business. It's better to label it 'spirituality'. That makes exploring the amount of compassion and sympathy in intentions and decisions of directors, owners or leaders a bit more accessible. Today, the left half of our brain (analytic, performance management, total quality, numbers, strategic planning, compliance management, models, structures, profit goals etc.), may be combined with the right half (creativity, spaciousness, intentions, feeling, intuition, transparency, vulnerability, values, meaning, atmosphere etc.) This love thing isn't exactly new (just like nothing will ever be truly new, except for the always surprising ways of love), because even in the 18th and 19th century, large undertakings have been started based on spirituality. Think of Cadbury Rowntree by the Quakers.

Spiritual

It will be the task of managers and leaders to make their own unique translation of spirituality in the coming years, one that works in their surroundings, service offer and organization. The time has come and the necessity grows. For personal gains and designing efficient processes, procedures, protocols and business models. Just imagine the new meeting agenda of the future!

Barbara Heyn sees more and more intercultural teams from around the world working together, which requires an emphatic ability anyway (to be able to achieve results). Those cultural differences necessitate openness and awareness of each others 'core values' and differing perceptions of reality (else you will not be able to communicate). And principles of durability such as 'people, planet, profit' require ethical decisions about what is good and what is wrong, in order to establish new commitment based on the heart and on spiritual connections.

Religion, relation

Based on the Christian reformed denomination many aren't (yet) completely used to experiencing personal feeling as a God given gift on which mankind is allowed and able to rely on and belief in. Authenticity is often limited to a superficial fashion fad, made up by marketeers or worldly psychologists. Still, authentic faith (and living by it) is something that the faithful can learn to appreciate, exactly because it comes so very close to your own, personal relationship with Jesus. When you experience the inner peace of Christ and you are allowed to feel the inner calm that He provides (for instance from the greeting/blessing votum with which the service in Church starts and ends), this is often still a feeling people want to distrust. Believers cannot accept their own senses as sanctifying, valuable or as a leading principle in order to become a 'new' human being. Because this might mean that you try to find security and salvation within you (eat this apple and 'become a God yourself', the serpent told Eve) and not by the sacrifice and suffering of Christ. It is a complex matter.

> *Neither shall they say, See here! or, see there! for,*
> *behold, the kingdom of God is within you.*
> *(Jesus, Luke 17)*

A lot of authentic humanness is lost when we keep distrusting ourselves and keep shutting off 'our own senses'. Evangelic reborn Christians have a head start there, although they lack a firm theoretical basis (why can't it ever be easy!). Believing is still a matter of 'being rationally cognitive certain' too often and not enough 'trusting your senses, feelings', based on an inner conviction. Being able to identify and 'find' yourself in Christ is also a matter of discovering your authenticity and uniqueness. Also as a Christian. Provided of course there is a balance between ratio and emotion. Between knowing and feeling. Between inside and outside. Between what has been given to you from above and what is of the planet surface to be responsible for in this universal, magic, indeed wonderful relation between Creator and those created.

> *Holy words long preserved / for our walk in this world,*
> *They resound with God's own heart. / Oh let the ancient*
> *words impart Words of Life, words of Hope / Give us*
> *strength, help us cope In this world, where we roam /*
> *Ancient words will guide us Home. Ancient words ever*
> *true / Changing me and changing you, We have*
> *come with open hearts / Oh let the ancient words impart*
> *Holy words of our Faith / Handed down to this age*
> *Came to us through sacrifice / Oh heed the faithful words*
> *of Christ. Holy words long preserved / For our walk*
> *in this world. They resound with God's own heart /*
> *Oh let the ancient words impart. (M.W. Smith)*

Authenticity in religion is, if you ask me, to continue letting go of fear and despair and find a personal freedom and connectedness with and in Christ (through trial and error). Feeling counts. This results in letting go of 'the old me' and 'what belongs to this world', in order to subsequently be able to take on and fulfill a more servant attitude. Authenticity is overwhelmingly beautiful and very valuable. Especially Christian leaders and especially reformed managers, focused on their logic, dogma's and knowledge, should understand that and embrace it as an addition on their rich traditions and valuable doctrines.

Motivating

Love and spirituality have a lot to do with motivation and change. When leaders wonder how they can motivate and bind people again, the key can be found in increasing trust and hope. Everything that really, deeply and intrinsically motivates people to perform better, show more initiative, be more involved, remain courageous and determined, keep doing the right thing and go along with changes comes … from the source of spirituality. Than mankind will seek true contact and find the issues and solutions that will truly help people, based on realization of equality, faith and relevance.

That is where we are going. Whether you find it soft, a dream, unrealistic, 'bla bla' or 'inappropriate' or 'invented elsewhere': please get used to it and adapt. It isn't a matter of 'just thinking of a new model' or starting another taskforce. You'll first have to find out what drives and motivates you. Cooperate; be in charge and control also based on of soul & heart. It really does open up a new world of opportunities (and appreciation). Think of all the youngsters and their drives, which will man your institution soon and will put your vision and mission and ideas into effect in the future.

> *What the heart gives away is never gone …*
> *It is kept in the hearts of others. (Robin St. John)*

Out of love!

'Love management' has only one goal: making others happy. It is a simple and fascinating need in our lives (think of Dutch TV shows like Opsporing Verzocht, Memories, and Boer Zoekt Vrouw). All we have to do now is to wait for the first top manager who is courageous enough to break the taboo and who will state, as a leader, that he acts out of love for the wellbeing of others. This will bring about great exposure and positive energy!

As a small step towards this moment, product selling will become helping, facilitating and assisting. Sharon Drew Morgan looks at it this way: in order to be able to take a decision to purchase something, entirely without being forced to do so, we will learn to connect and coach instead of persuade and (subconsciously) manipulate. That will be the new approach. Display your broad expertise and personal opinion instead of your narrow, scary self-interest and personal urge to score your own points for the good of you only.

> *Coaching is unlocking a person's potential to maximize their own performance. It is helping them to learn rather than teaching them. (Timothy Gallwey)*

Buyers, consumers make decisions based on needs, but especially based on durability and on retention of value as well. This requires a different leadership mentality. From chain efficiency and financial profit, towards addressing problems as questions, stimulate awareness and assist people to decide together (even about your wish to specifically buy your products, to embrace your point of view). Allow them (the eventual buyers, influencers and opinion leaders) to see where you solve which peril with their money or time. Buyers' motives will become much more important than sellers' motives. Sellers become 'decision consultants'. Authentic communication is the secret ingredient, offline and online.

Your vision will become clear only when you can look into your own heart. Who looks outside, dreams; who looks inside, awakens. (Carl Jung)

Personal note

Can any 'normal', educated, friendly motivated human being ever meet all these qualities and characteristics? What kind of superhuman effort is required? One must almost be a saint to become a leader who is authentic, morally just and driven to serve mankind. Yes, I can imagine it seems that way. Because, deep down inside us we all miss the real, pure, genuine commitment to first serve others and to refrain from any greed and selfishness. This almost asks for and implies a connection with a Higher Authority, Divinity and loving Spirit. As a Christian and Bible reader I try to follow Christ (as very authentic leader). Of course also other (spiritual) sources and beliefs allow personal authenticity to grow for the benefit of all. I wish its roots were founded in love and not hate or destruction; in light and not in darkness. Embrace SQ (Spiritual Intelligence) as your new state of mind. Rethink the meaning of 'human-unity' and your relation and contact to the Whole. When the world around you is in chaotic turmoil, when all certainties fall away, when complete silence overtakes all the distracting noises, when your carefully collected possessions are taken away, when you existence becomes insecure, when love leaves you … you will turn inwards and re-find your connection with nature and the Divine. Accepting this, might already help you (and me) 'to connect' without any personal, economic or worldwide disasters happening first.

Joost Gerrits (Leadership study 2009): 'To me the definition of authentic leadership is: knowing who you are and how you come across. With high standards for yourself, for what you provide to this world and for the world you would want to live in.'

10.

Authentic Communications

Based on the many forms of communication (advertising, information, external or internal communication, PR, PA, marketing communication, publicity, personal recruitment communications and financial, investor communication, issue and (online) network communication, social communication, propaganda, etc), I made the choice of only discussing the corporate communication and in particular the mechanisms of influence and manipulation.

Corporate communication represents the singularity and translates the identity and values of an organization. It stands for messaging and matters such as the desired image you want stakeholders to perceive you through, or the bonding of relations or informing interested parties or the way consumers experience your (desirable, sympathetic) reputation. The personal aspects of authentic communication, through leaders, owners, managers, politicians or board members themselves, have already been covered in the previous chapters.

If the organization is already perceived authentic, then the control of the communication should also be based on authenticity.

That is considered an optimal start. If the organization isn't seen as authentic – and the communicative aspects such as setting goals, intentions, wanted results, tone of voice, campaign planning, ideas and media choices are still based on conventional values –, it's impossible for the communication to come across as truly and sincerely authentic. That is, unless the responsible communication director is personally authentic and thus has an authentic influence on the tone, the choice of media and the appeal of the communication.

> *Self-expression must pass into communication for its fulfillment. (Pearl S. Buck)*

Origin

The essence of the words 'authentic' and 'communication' are popular again, especially with respect to the old Greek meaning. The words can be traced back to the Latin 'communicatio', as well as to the Greek word 'communis'. Communicatio stands for 'to inform, and is thus more related to processes and the technical aspects of communication. Communis means 'being connected' and is thus more related to the social aspect, community and desired effect of 'Communications'. Both perspectives require your attention towards authentic communications, in which social connectivity within and from authentic organizations are considered quite important. Speaking of Greeks and, in particular, Aristotle, the means of the speaker (or a communicating institution) to convince others are: conviction because of the personality of the speaker (or organization); conviction because the public's (or target group's, stakeholder's) emotions are addressed (or their perception of values); or by the text spoken (the message, medium or the content), if it is based on the truth or on convincing arguments. Put in authentic words and intentions: how you perceive the world and its meaning,

and convince others by:
- Logos: that what you say is true, sensible and consistent
- Ethos: that which you offer is of value to you and to others
- Pathos: you stand for that which you offer and you are able to 'sell' it with heart and soul.

> *Our chief want in life is someone who*
> *will make us do what we can. (Emerson)*

Communicating authentically isn't a trick, technique or fashion fad. Even now, books and articles are published stating that authenticity is an old hype and marketing issue because of its temporary popularity. That means to me that its meaning and influence hasn't been fully understood yet.

Intrinsic

Authenticity is not like an external, handy and instrumental 'coat' to be put on or taken off when it's raining or sunny outside, it is an inner 'state of mind'. Shrugging it away as a temporary phenomenon is nearly the same as saying that acquired wisdom will disappear through time; that eating food daily is, in fact, unnecessary; that breathing is needless or that spirituality will heal by itself. How can you not want to become (more) authentic? Who wants to voluntarily live in 'the matrix of fake', in a system forced upon you by 'others', full of deceit and lies? Sure, some people will want to live that way and flourish by abuse. Yes, there will be always a few unfortunately.

> *Have the courage to say no. Have the courage*
> *to face the truth. Do the right thing because it is right.*
> *Theses are the magic keys to living your life with*
> *Integrity. (W. Clement Stone)*

Using authenticity in marketing or communication (because it is 'hip' and people will be more receptive to it, or because only profit figures will rise faster) will be instantly noticeable in daily life. 'Being genuine' will, for instance, be translated as 'retro'. That can also be found in the many newly designed old cars and the tendency towards retrieving and adjusting 'traditions' from past decades and in the peddling of 'honest craftsmanship' or 'grandma's recipe'. Being cynical a little: people used to be simpler (mentally) an strangely old fashioned compared to or modern, efficient, smart society of today; they even mechanically typed A4 sheets of texts with carbon paper in between for copying and actually found time to spend with their children and give attention to family matters and principles of living together. Sure!

Value driven attitude

No, authentic communication should be based on the foundations, motives and values of the organization. The history, backgrounds and the corporate story are of great importance in order to know what you 'value' and on what kind of origin the institution is founded. For instance: the 'Founding Fathers' in politics still have great influence in the USA.

Keep busy then, also with respect for the efforts of earlier generations. Making a corporate story (visually and cinematic) has made its comeback: where did it all begin, with what kind of passion did it start and what motives drove the original entrepreneur or founder, what did he hold on to, what 'golden rules' were followed, why was product 'x' invented and why did it became a success as well? How did the offer establish and why did people remain so attached and connected to the company culture?

> *Half of the work that is done in this world is*
> *to make things appear what they are not.*
> *(E. R. Beadle)*

Communication specialists and agencies are modernizing value driven concepts in order to enable people to connect again to strategies and goals, increase acceptance and allow organizations - based on their services or brands- being better seen, heard, felt and smelt. An entire authentic world (of experience) is built around institutions again. Products marketed are again an expression and extension of the organization's personality. Positioning is based on servant ship again, and also based on purpose and relevance. It's less about the intrinsic qualities of a product (who still looks under the hood buying a new car?) and more about the desired (side-) effects of use and application.

Words like practicality and composition are enriched with emotional values like meaning, purpose, and atmosphere in advertising. The degree of authenticity of an advertising manager, designer or copywriter will be taken into account during audits performed by the (authentic) client. It's becoming a criteria for selection.

Other accents

Imagine: a non authentic, but brilliant, famous and creative advertisement couple will not be able to understand what has suddenly 'got hold' of their client, when he rejects their concepts and propositions or removes his companies' account somewhere else. They thought it was all about scoring turnover, seducing customers and stand out between the crowd as much as possible and about 'sales leads and likeability' and such. Well, yes, these criteria will stay but all those come second or third, behind authenticity.

First it's about: showing respect (no hidden manipulators and subluminal messages or small print at the backside or bottom) and presenting a truthful and honest picture (does this car really drive 20 km to the liter as stated in the brochure? Or only in a test simulation and not in real life while driving on the highway with 2 passengers?). From now on, it's all about an upright selection of information, finding 'the benefit' and 'the promise'... based on care and honesty. Please.

Avoid the harsh manipulation based on unproven subjective claims ('it will make you look younger') or fear ('get insurance for the uncertain future ... now') or false happiness (the smiling, happy, slim standard models everywhere). It shouldn't be about honeying the mouth and constant exaggerated product pushing and excessive brutal promotions anymore, but about having the courage to illustrate and determine what are the benefits as well as the lesser flipsides in your offer. The loudmouthed tone and sensationalism will naturally fade away in the media and messaging.

> *The truth is more important than the facts. (Frank Lloyd Wright)*

Consider this website text for the Dow Jones Sustainability index:
> 'Increasingly, investors are diversifying their portfolios by investing in companies that set industry-wide best practices with regard to sustainability. Two factors drive this development. First, the concept of corporate sustainability is attractive to investors because it aims to increase long-term shareholder value. Second, sustainability leaders are increasingly expected to show superior performance and favourable risk/return profiles. A growing number of investors is convinced that sustainability is a catalyst for enlightened and disciplined management, and, thus, a crucial success factor. Leading sustainability companies display high levels of competence in addressing global and industry challenges in a variety of areas:
> 1. Strategy: Integrating long-term economic, environmental and social aspects in their business strategies while maintaining global competitiveness and brand reputation.

2. Financial: Meeting shareholders' demands for sound financial returns, long-term economic growth, open communication and transparent financial accounting.
3. Customer & Product: Fostering loyalty by investing in customer relationship management and product and service innovation that focuses on technologies and systems, which use financial, natural and social resources in an efficient, effective and economic manner over the long-term.
4. Governance and Stakeholder: Setting the highest standards of corporate governance and stakeholder engagement, including corporate codes of conduct and public reporting.
5. Human: Managing human resources to maintain workforce capabilities and employee satisfaction through best-in-class organisational learning and knowledge management practices and remuneration and benefit programs'
(Dow Jones Indexes and SAM launched the Dow Jones Sustainability Indexes (DJSI).

I regard this initiative and these criteria as a prelude to authenticity as the next driver for defining profit & reward. New communicational planning will be about 'being a part of something and a network' and as a sender: about facilitating and providing (online and offline) that need. It will be about the 'use' of things and the 'purpose' of products as well as the added value (to your happiness, peace, harmony or bond) of your unique points of view (or acquisitions or joint ventures). That doesn't automatically mean that marketing communications has to become all fluffy while e.g. filming commercials on green, open pastures, inhabited by butterflies and accompanied by frolicking hippies. No, it can also be done in a businesslike manner and sober and, if need be, in a minimalist setting with the most modern facilities, insights and media.

Use of language

The use of promotional language has been heavily studied and reviews, experiences, advertisement headings are still often written for one purpose: attraction attention. It often has nothing to do with the language, sentences and words we -the people- use at home or in our workplace. Language in adverts is used to sell or emphasize the pleasant sides and praise products, often through the use of stereotypes. There's nothing wrong with that, but it often isn't the authentic language we ourselves speak on a normal day or when we want to communicate personal information.

> *The basic tool for the manipulation of reality is the manipulation of words. If you can control the meaning of words, you can control the people who must use the words. (Philip K. Dick)*

Advertising language plays with our emotions, unconsciousness, prejudices and opinions and forces us to think in one direction while any creative double meaning of suggestion made, is sometimes hard to understand for a lot of consumers. If you use 'real' language and stop 'putting words in peoples mouths' on behalf of someone famous or deliberately conceal negative characteristics, the creative twist in a header or playful tension might decline a bit, but the bond with the readers and the credibility of the sender will increase.

> *The difference between fiction and reality is that fiction has to make sense. (Tom Clancy)*

Different Umfeld

By now, users, consumers and clients witness the contradictions in our world and how big a price the planet, environment and climate have to pay, how large internationals operate, based on which motives and how they even exploit people to make a small group richer. People have become skeptical and cynical and demand to know what happens to their food, what goes into (or doesn't anymore) into products and what products are exactly made of. Organizations have to answer for social and surrounding issues, for matters such as honest trade and origin. Consumers ask: who and what makes 'the difference' at, with and by your institution?

Organizations are becoming sensitive again to conscious consumerism and buying boycotts. Consumers, constituents and target groups members are becoming citizens, neighbors, peers, inhabitants and ... humans again. That alone is already a step forward. Based on the need for transparency, a sensible, clear connection is needed between expenses, destination and experiences (through, e.g. cases, meetings, stories and such) in authentic communication.

There is a need for an appealing story, the 'his-story', starting from the very beginning of the company. All the choices once made will be illustrated, successes evaluated, reevaluated and valued based on the current core values. Mistakes and failures are known and consequences will be illustrated by means of the lessons learned. Exaggeration or use of fear and negativity is seldom a way, choice or option. Words like positive, pleasant and sober, however, are.

The turnover

Organizations are always (consciously or unconsciously) working on their reputation. It's the way shareholders see, experience and value the organization. It is the entire impression that employees, customers, clients, the press, politics and the surroundings have (gotten) of you. A reputation says something about the measure of connectedness with the surrounding. Authentic organizations do no longer use their means of communication, products and behavior for a cosmetic approach anymore, but rather for a sincere one and a value based presentation, based on inner convictions.

Every employee is able to influence this image.

> *The shortest and surest way to live with honor in the world is to be in reality what we would appear to be. (Socrates)*

The corporate image is just a bit different from a corporate reputation. The image is the mental picture people have of a certain organization or person or brand, whether internal or external; offline or online. No one needs to have had a relationship of some kind with that organization or her representatives. It is possible, but not necessary. Building reputations requires more time, for 'something' has to be proven.

Based on consistent and reliable performance, sincere economical participation and by suitable communications 'from the heart'.

Sensitive example
Mignon van Halderen (ERIM) studied at the social and politically sensitive oil industry, how management compromise between staying competitive and remaining authentic. She studies the corporate communication of six major oil companies, namely Shell, BP, Exxon, Chevron, Statoil and Petrobras. The giants have to distinguish themselves in order to become appealing, but at the same time they must also remain authentic, transparent and consistent in order to inspire trust. Oil companies often try to distinguish themselves by expression specific points of view with respect to the current social-political matters, such as the problem of global warming. They try to communicate a clear vision in order to claim 'mental leadership' that way.

The art of authenticity is to show that this is more than just a PR technique. It's firstly about internal anchorage. The ERIM study indicates that stakeholders judge a company more positive if they have the idea that the company is authentic, transparent and consistent in its communication. It's more important for companies to inspire trust (be authentic), than it is to be different.

> *Authenticity is most important*
> *for determining your reputation*
> *(Cees van Riel)*

Strategic issue
Dutch professor Cees van Riel has succeed in bringing the matter of reputation management and the importance of communication to the top, higher up the organizational hierarchy. He analyses and combines the assessments of stakeholders (investors, clients, employees, pubic) on six different aspects:

1. Emotional Appeal
   (like, trust, respect)
2. Products & Services
   (strong brand, innovative, quality, values)
3. Vision & Leadership
   (inspiring vision, strong leadership, clear values)
4. Workplace Environment
   (attractive appealing workplace, well managed, talent development)
5. Financial Performance
   (past results, low risk, growth perspectives, recognize opportunities)
6. Social Responsibility
   (citizenship, environmental stewardship, ethics).

Consistent image building and reputation management is usually ruined by internal tribalism and ego tripping. In order to excel in the area of reputations, there are five matters to take into account

(Van Riel): Visibility, Consistency, Transparency, Distinctiveness and ... Authenticity.

> *Executive's good intentions and words, like their companies' stocks, lose their value when nothing backs them up. (Al Watts)*

The RepTrack ™ method measures how organizations are experienced by (primary) stakeholders or assessed on matters such as:
- Products and services *(quality, price/performance, expertise and customer orientation)*
- Innovation and renovation *(ability to adjust – market orientation)*
- Working environment *(rewards, development, wellbeing)*
- Governance *(honesty, transparency, ethics)*
- Society *(influence on society, social involvement, awareness of surroundings and environment)*
- Performance *(continuity, focused on results, recognizes opportunities)*
- Leadership *(clear vision, excellent management, inspiring, well organized and ... authentic)*

Mazutis & Slawinski (2008) argue that authentic leadership can foster a dialogue that is self aware, balanced, congruent and transparent. Authentic dialogue can stimulate learning at all levels of an organization and open opportunities to create new understanding rather than approach differences through power struggles.

Organizing opinions
Information (including the truth) can be massaged in such a way, so it sounds more 'pleasant'. Agencies often do things like this in the interest of the sender, sponsor or provider. We call this 'spin'. It's the sensitive side of communication and PR.

Of course, also conventional advertising, promotion or communication is often a matter of choosing and selecting information. So, your 'own' conclusion, opinion or perception as a reader is sometimes created based on what is NOT mentioned … but as such interpreted or understood. From an authentic point of view regarding this phenomenon; it is all about what choices are made why, who makes it and based on what conviction.

> *To separate the purpose of a business from the purpose*
> *of people who are in the business is, I think,*
> *not a good thing. (Michael Josephson)*

By now, we've all already been conditioned and programmed -as consumers and users- by the media and manipulative selective use of text and images. We barely realize (let alone: feel) with what we are connected en actually believe that we, for instance, are able to become immune to disease and misery through the use of (poisonous) vaccinations. We now believe that financial debt is actually a form of fiscal deductable property. We really believe that stock market prices reflect trades and are the consequence of supply and demand.

Our ability of perception and self-consciousness are being tested by the pre-prepared, pre-selected and fully managed coverage, smoke curtains and opinion influencing journalism en corporate media giants. The abundance and complexity of information and events is confusing and we blindly follow the choices, opinions and selections of so-called experts, scientist, spin-doctors and opinion leaders.

> *Life is the continuous adjustment of internal relations*
> *to external relations. (Herbert Spencer)*

How do authentic companies deal with this? A number of thoughts to hold on to:

- Communicate using more facts and logic and less by playing people's emotion.
- Allow more 'genuine' people to speak for you and less expert opinions.
- Tell the advantages as well as the disadvantages; don't just create a 'mood'.
- Use less fake language and constructed words for 'unique' ingredients or 'special' additions, predicting groundbreaking effects.
- Speak using positive, clear words and less generalizations, commonplaces and veiled lines.
- Make sure employees truly support the company. Hiring celebrities or artists is allowed, but only if the proposition and this person are approved internally as well, not because some expensive famous face will just increase sales based on paid for credibility.
- Offer room for and be open minded to irritation, complaints or unpleasant experiences and do not play it down or make a fool out of yourself by only ridiculously avoiding it, unilaterally emphasizing the benefits, faking denial and surprise or by belittling the credibility and dignity of other party.
- Always be ready to be held responsible for the course and ethical choices, despite of the mockery, daily fads or moral judgment.
- Respect emotion, conviction and opinions and do not automatically invalidate these matters because of their unverifiable scientific and technological research (of vague, distant sources).

Manipulation

No one escapes from it. No one is able to shut it out for 100%. In the end, it is the core of all communication, no matter out of what pure motive or impure intention.

Based on wanting to realize more profit or wanting to share feelings and get comforted. Manipulation is the reason of entrepreneurship, education, determination of value, loving, talking, evangelizing, acting and reacting, consuming and offering support. It consists of our entire behavior.

> The leader for today and the future will be focused
> on how to be, how to develop quality, character,
> mind-set, values, principles and courage.
> (Frances Hesselbein)

The measure of influence a corporation wants to exercise or a person wants to have, can be a conscious strategy. Obtaining insights in how this works increases your personal freedom of choice, independence and tenability. Besides, authentic enterprises are just like 'real' enterprises, which resort to all available methods and techniques in order to justify their existence and increase their influence on the outside world. In order to promote the free choice and free will of people and minimize the manipulative influence allows me to venture further into this phenomenon. Robert Cialdini wrote about influence in his influential book 'Influence'. I've taken the liberty of adding some perspectives and my own findings to his most important conclusions.

Mutuality
Giving away something (small) obligates nearly every receiver to do something in return. Wanting to live up to that is nearly a psychological law. Owing somebody something (so to speak) is an obligate feeling. The same holds true for making concessions and receiving them in order to acquire, for instance, group commitment. Hence that we often get invited to accept a business gift, or the free flyer offered to you on the street, or 'click here' to accept an online newsletter 'with no strings attached', or accept a free quick scan by

a consultancy or participate in an online test... etc.

> *When one is out of touch with oneself, one cannot touch others. (Anne Morrow Lindbergh)*

Commitment

When we have finally decided for a reasoned point of view, we often go to great lengths (based on a human need to come across as being consistent) to secure that view or opinion, sometimes against our better judgment. When you have committed yourself, your commitment will be valid even if the circumstances have long since changed or do not apply anymore. This can bring about (quite some) social pressure. The pressure can be identified by the little voice in your head or the feeling in your stomach or by listening to your heart. You will be remembered and called upon because you once committed yourself to something, but you 'feel' that 'something isn't right' anymore. Especially if you already experienced some doubt when you committed yourself in the first place. Therefore it might be useful to ask yourself: If I'd known what I know now, would I have made the same concession, promise or commitment? Reviewing the situation with fresh eyes, by means of this question, will lessen the manipulating, straining effect immediately. Think of the organizations that call upon you, just because you've made a choice in favor of them or their product. Your loyalty will of course be rewarded with discounts and such.

Consistency

People within organizations, and therefore their leaders as well, have the tendency to want to be consistent in their words, behavior and conviction, because it is greatly appreciated and makes you recognizable. Consistency also counts as a major benefit because it enables you to quickly make decisions based on credible experiences, and saves you the hassle of constantly checking or researching everything relating to the company in question.

> *Trickery and treachery are the practices of fools that have not the wits enough to be honest.*
> *(Benjamin Franklin)*

The danger of manipulation during consent, as well as during consistency, is in the repetition. After the first occasion you made a stand, people tend to agree quicker with offers or request that resemble that first one, the first time they made their decision. As supplier you'll be able to influentially manipulate while buyers make their first stand, already knowing in advance what you'll ask for the future (and getting it done a lot easier).

This is because people are led by that first promise, concession or way they acted once. You'll recognize it when it you're being involved in something, one step at a time, first by 'just' looking at some picture or confirming an innocent participation, by being allowed to read a page in advance or by answering a simple first question in a survey. One well-known method is to be handed a free newspaper in the street, and to then feel like you're obligated to stop and listen to their offer for a subscription.

Peer pressure
In order to discover what is valuable, or what is the truth, what is wise and useful, we watch and listen to others. It's something no one escapes from, for it's something we all did in our education and upbringing, we all learned from e.g. our parents. When others, who are close or familiar to us, set an example, we mirror our own behavior to theirs. This principle can be used to quicken someone's assent on the basis of the fact that many other people (especially acquaintances or opinion leaders) have already preceded you. This makes the decision a lot easier to make, it seems.

While at the same time the one who decides on basis of this, is very vulnerable to unwanted manipulation by means of peer pressure.

> *Leadership is based on inspiration, not domination; on cooperation, not intimidation. (William Arthur Ward)*

When trying to imagine these temptations, think of (free… uhem… alert!) conferences, bus trips and sightseeing with travel groups or free introductions for e.g. motivational trainings. Insecurity forces us to lean on others, and the same goes for equality, wanting to be equal to the other. So please, always keep thinking for yourself, as an authentic – if need be, contraire- person and do not let anything knock you off by 'proof' provided by 'experts' who of course also use or have bought 'it'. If they play by the number, through the use of lines such as 'many people already preceded you' or: 'already thousands of applications received before 18:00 hrs', or 'thousands of fellow-inhabitants already joined in' … you now know what manipulation is taking place in your head.

Attractive

If you like or know others, you're more likely to give in go them. Sympathy may be enhanced artificially. Making people physically more attractive (beautiful people automatically have a head start and get 'it' done quicker) or making things look nicer, or window dress issues, has become a special trade lots of professionals practice, from photo shoppers up and to spin doctors and lobbyists. Wag the dog! We find it pleasant when people look just like us and we instantly become less judicial. It's the same when we are praised a lot and thanked exuberantly. Our independent decision-making and intuitive resistance collapses and we become more compliant on the spot. Services and products are therefore consciously associated with positive events, stories or testimonials. It just sells a lot better than the sober assessment between positive and negative, good and evil, true of false.

> *Every man has three characters – that which he exhibits,*
> *that which he has, and that which he thinks he has. (Karr)*

It isn't for nothing these professionals mention the dangers or warnings, just in a flash and right at the last second of e.g. the radio commercial (for instance that smoking kills and loaning money costs money). The same goes again: if you know how the manipulation works, it's already less effective and you'll look at that beautiful, pleasantly smiling model with her bright white teeth and unbelievable voluminous hair, claiming she (meaning you, with your balding head, full of dry dull dying hair) 'is worth' or 'deserves' this shampoo. By paying more attention to what is said exactly and by actually thinking for yourself () when advertisers claim dermatologists have 'looked' at it (the intention is, of course, that you think 'studied and approved it' and thus 'its safe and smart'). Something you'll often see on web shops is: forward it to X for free or let Y know about this. A tip or 'retweet' from an (acquired) friend of 'follower' works also and after all is even more positive and thus… more manipulative.

Authority
Stanley Milgram thinks of obedience as a means of pressuring you into compliance, if that obedience is demanded of you by an authority, based on our assumption that they must be a bit more right than you are yourselves or probably have more knowledge or insight than we do. Besides, we react more to the (self appointed, designated or chosen) authority than we react on the contents of a message. That is the influential effect. We fall for the symbolism, titles, uniforms, stage setting, status and large … you name it (from podiums, egos and cars up and to large houses and crowds).

In order to not being manipulated, you must find true, substantial expertise and concrete answers (But how? But when? But which?) and check the credibility and trustworthiness, especially when senders first concede something to you out of tactical deliberations or even exercise some initial soft self critique at the beginning of an interview or commercial in order to strengthen an (fake) impression of honesty and integrity. The (mis-)use of borrowed authority can be found everywhere (from hallmarks up and to assessment marks or reviewing points given to something).

The clever shortage

People appreciate something that is in short supply or that is hard to come by more. Something that is rare, must have more quality. Antique and older art is often more expensive. The agency that announces that they're not taking any new clients must be very special, if it hasn't got any time anymore for new assignments. Limited editions are more expensive. An expiration date or 'only 3 crazy discount days' attracts a lot of people and forces them to decide in a hurry. Restrictions in time and freedom function like a red rag, it makes you desire it even more.

> *Just get rid of the false and you will automatically realize the true. (Ho-Shan)*

Selective entry, rising levels of authority, limited editions and the stamp that says 'confidential information' manipulates us already by being organized or naming it that way. If, next to scarcity, competition also comes in, we become more and more accessible to manipulation and start to think less and less clearly. The antidote is to take a step back and ask yourself what you think you really need. It'll probably be a lot less. Does it say: 'only two pieces left'? Or: 'just an hour to go?' Remain sober and consider whether that, which you experience a shortage now, is really what is says it is.

Authentic organizations and their marketing and communication departments also influence us. My wish is that they focus less on the effect, on the deception and on the manipulation, and allow their relations to make a choice out of their own free will. No matter how subjective those notions really are. The servant leaders handle them with care and because they want to be at other people's service. The idea that you have to 'stimulate' people to buy your product or adopt your ideas and that you have to 'play' their 'latent' needs is becoming more and more unethical and will be avoided in the long authentic run.

Seducing

You can also choose to be brief and concise in your communication. It works fine as well and has nothing secretly to it. A different way to draw attention is e.g. to hire a well-groomed, sympathetic senior, it doesn't have to be the ever young, handsome, funny and successful model. Sexy still sells very well (think of all the TV music channels, videos, and magazine covers and trade fairs). Being able to make some extra money all the time is one of those typical Dutch national characteristics. If you get the idea of (being able to) win something or getting something for 'free', our logic and ratio is instantly hidden away and we react by instinct. More for the same price, free sample, discount sales, discount groceries, large and small prizes at games ... it might be a good idea to also think about the benefit for the other inhabitants of this world instead of thinking only about satisfying our own greed.

> *If we attach more importance to what other people believe than to what we know to be true - if we value belonging over being – we will not attain authenticity. (Nathaniel Branden)*

Appealing to health or ills also produces good results most of the time. By being able to prevent illness, stress or loss of hair or any sign of old age etc. Abusing our sensitivity to status is a well-known manipulator. We want better, newer, sharper, bigger and flatter things than our colleagues or neighbors. An authentic human often realizes this is one of the first mental effects he dearly wants to keep away from. This also includes the (improper) use of hidden messages, editing of images or biophilia (does have an edge, however, as an authentic manipulator), exaggerated emotions (someone has to cry on this television show) and playing with exaggerations (tabloids) or moods (being happy is: getting flowers, felicity is: getting a diamond, love is: getting a golden ring etc.) will change towards a more authentic associating, such as with nature, the climate, saving energy, unity, spirituality and care for our environment.

These last issues are being regarded more and more as something authentic. Luring and seducing people into your camp by 'influencing' them in 'finely tuned' ways are OUT. It will be done by 'involving' them and finding a way to appeal to the buyers by presenting your identity and singularity and by facilitating and bonding groups of people based on your vision and values, as a producer or service organization. By letting people think along and participate, by letting them help build something and letting them join the ongoing innovative conversation. The new social media, virtual networks and online possibilities offer more than enough opportunities for this.

In conclusion
Being authentic means that behavior becomes more natural and is more consistent with you. Masks may be taken off a little; our hearts and left hemispheres may participate hand in hand with our rational, numerical sides. It's also about letting go of 'more, more and more' possessions, fear, greed and egocentric motives (to own

'things' or money yourself). You will truly see other people again and want to help them when needed. This aid is given with your belief that having 'enough' is more than sufficient. Additionally you will succeed in discovering the good in everything, even in suffering and pain and shortage. Those do not disappear, but their duration seems shorter for some strange reason. It also has to do with the inner peace of acceptance. Note: not from laziness or indolence.

Authentic managers are responsible people who radiate positivism and hope.' Next to that, you'll always be able to see the bright side of things even while experiencing suffering, You become authentic by taking a break first, pause, come into contact with your soul, think about what you want, what occupies your mind and motivate you while you let go of the temptation and fears of this world and dare to trust on the Higher Force and subsequently on your own strength and unique contribution. From now on, you'll only make choices based on that and find work that really suit you and no slave labor, which you only accept in order to pay your mortgage.

Authenticity is an issue for daydreamers and New Age enlightened thinkers. Definitely! But also for sharp rational scientific managers and factual business analysts and sober rationalists. Because they might - not yet by themselves - notice and observe through others (and results and figures), that large target groups, customers and opinion leaders are willing to pay for authenticity and integrity. In addition to a pleasant experience, a certain belief, an inner peace, a clear sense of destination ... authenticity is also a very rational issue to survive in a new commercial era to come.

The benefits reflect a new pleasure resulting from working together, a fairer image building, initiatives being discussed, a strong community feeling, more personal satisfaction, initiatives and commitment. And less absenteeism, lower marketing and recruitment costs, more 'power' through the alignment of personal and corporate interests and a better balance between private and working conditions. The old mentality to earn as much as possible with a minimum amount of effort is now obsolete. Instead one wishes to deliver an optimal contribution in all-important roles in life for a fair compensation. Excellent performance will be rewarded accordingly. But everyone will determine what is regarded as excellent. I'm not looking for a completely balanced society, but a transparent one with more involvement

It actually concerns all organizations and institutions dealing with clients, customers, consumers, voters, users or members. I see commercial companies as a precursor of change towards CA, because they are alert where new opportunities and markets and the future behavior of customer groups and networks are concerned. But I could be wrong. I like to be surprised by those who pick up the gauntlet first. Perhaps it's the small independent professional or the owner with 5 regional vegetable stores, a dental practice or a small financial consultancy firm. It's not exclusively confined to big, large companies.

Not all employees will always be benefitted. But more and more will submerge and become committed again. They want to become stronger and more independent, energetic and motivated and stop with delivering minimal results within the safe limits of narrow task descriptions. Who dares to give themselves again – slowly - and will employ their talents - after receiving some appreciation for their performances - and sense new room for making errors. They experience a new confidence because they are respected for what they are and want and will contribute.'

As a CEO you will become more Corporate Authentic based on an inner reflection and as a result of changed external conditions and a new economic reality and atmosphere. Because your authentic core values will determine the degree of trust given to you and because your future employees already live and operate authentically different. Because the external customer base and network of relationships will rely on and relate to your new level of authenticity (and that of your organization). Because after this period of unbridled ego and super-capitalism, it is inevitable that we start restructuring our society again and learn to look inward and find out what excites, challenges and engages us to what is truly genuine and no longer fake.'

What organizations 'earn' with this is a lot. More confidence, credibility and involvement with and from people, both internally and externally. There is a unity of intention and action, goals and presentation and alignment with values and strategy. Authentic companies have a competitive edge, are widely recognized while people sympathize with them and like to buy their goods and accept their leaders' authority. Whether it's about a tangible product, a policy, a program, a process or a service. It's quite simple actually and extremely profitable ... there's more in a corporate lifespan than just earning the most money to enrich a few.'

Organizations consist of people. Fact! So instead of just looking at yourself individually, you now decide as a Management Team or Administration or Board to look at what binds you together, to rediscover what you all stand for and what you want to create and contribute together, in an authentic manner. Of course it helps if you already have some personal individual authenticity, so you understand each other better. Some will drop out. It's a drastic new course. But organizations are like a corporate personality, a unified body so to speak, with parts, disciplines and tasks, functions and talents. Somewhere earlier in this book it says: you'll be more authentic individually, being and working with others. I believe this.

The end

11.

Justification

Why did I write this book? I got the idea in December 2008, when I was busy considering repositioning my business. My company name (Peetzen Ltd.), presentation texts and website were quite a few years old by then and I was often asked 'what do you do exactly ' or 'are you an agency or a consultant?'

Now I know that it isn't very smart with respect to perception and acceptation to confront a prospect with ambiguity. People aren't able to place you in a box or genre and that is commercially awkward.

A period of reflection dawned: who am I, what do I want, what gives me energy and how to write that down. A more personal company name was the first result (PeterVanPeetzen) accompanied by a new logo and a new website with content I had written myself. As of February 2009 this second beginning became visually discernible and it seemed to be all set for a new round of business. However, because of economic crisis work sometimes fluctuated and I had time left to spend on reading and studying. Online, from one source and website to the other and back again. And then, after the summer of 2009 my eye caught two words: authenticity and organization. Then it came to me: these two words exactly matched my offer, feeling, intuition and the content of my websites. It was the missing banner on my ship. Those were the names of what I wanted to achieve with my work and energy.

Then came the drive for more information. Night after night I absorbed new information under this banner and the idea of summarizing all this information in the form of a book was something new for me. Besides, a book could also serve as a nice gift for my relations. Then they would know what I stood for and what I wanted to achieve, the foundation of my perspective on, and analyses of, every new corporate presentation, expression, corporate design, tool, campaign, advert, website, etcetera. So the resolve was there; the beginning was made. Nice stimulants as well as skeptical comments befell me. It didn't matter; I found my way. Then my life as a writer (including doubts about my writing capabilities) began. All the reasons to stop passed by.

Becoming personally convinced of something,
is more difficult than trying to prove something
scientifically (Pleu).

And now, after about twelve months it's finally finished in English. On the whole, it isn't science and most definitely not a breakthrough. But is it food for inspiration, reflection and that little bit of realization to go about things just a bit differently as a leader, manager, executive or if you're self-employed. I truly hope so!
I want organizations to present themselves in a credible and authentic way, in line with what they stand for. An important list to me is: equivalence + reciprocity + trustworthiness + passion + commitment + credibility + gratitude = benefits and profit for all. I have trouble with fake, sham, hypocrisy, imitation, manipulation

and injustice. You are unique; please behave as such. And please find out where your uniqueness can express itself and in what. Do not behave or communicate in another way, or more perfectly than you intrinsically are. In the end it's not about what you own or earn, but who you have become to others. Physical beauty as well as Corporate attraction is appealing to me, when combined with internalized authenticity for a charismatic appearance and selfless behavior.

Authenticity (and its leadership) is that people know their true nature, their essence of who they fundamentally are. And that they can translate it to what they say and what they do in action.
So, there is congruence in who you are inside and what is palpable on the outside, visible, and also is expressed in deeds. People can be very nice in their true nature, but if it is not visible in how they deal with the coffee lady, then it will buy them nothing (P. Assink in J.H.M. Gerrits study, 2009)

12.

About The Author

Peter Leuhof has a marketing and communication background. Based on his studies and experiences, he developed the specialism to transform the 'style of the house' into a fitting visual and textual corporate 'house style'.

For this reason he talked with a lot of managers (and employees) over the last 25 years about the core of their corporate existence, motives, values and Identities.

His interests and quest for what is authentic and 'genuine' started a lot earlier during his reformed Christian upbringing within an Orthodox Church community. He always found the difference between the preached coming of the heavily kingdom versus the human (group-)behavior of the (un)religious people on this earth extremely interesting. Searching for what is sacred and what is sanctimonious, what is dogma versus experience, what is confessed versus what is done and what is religion versus relation?

Leuhof is hired by principals through his own company PeterVanPeetzen, to detect, bundle and strengthen the (already present) authenticity within organizations by means of the PVP

Authenticity Quickscan (pro) or the PVP Corporate Authenticity Register (pro). He analyses the status quo and offers advice about additional policy and improvements. Next to that he as a quest speaker inspires listeners to cooperate more authentically in their daily lives. He lives in The Netherlands, has been married over 22 years with his first wife Wilma and has 4 children.

So, after writing all this information on authenticity, did he become an authentic person? Is he an authentic husband to his wife? Is he an authentic father to his children? Is he an authentic leader for all his co-workers, or an authentic professional for his clients? Is he an authentic friend?

Peter: 'It is hard draw a final conclusion about that, myself. After all, truth lies in the eyes of the beholder. Genuineness is a lifetime struggle and I need others to help reflect and mirror my behavior and intentions. It requires meditation, reflection, disposition and praying and it takes practice to dismiss thoughts of e.g. selfishness and materialism. It's hard to say 'no' to buying or doing things just for the sake of being accepted by 'the group' and gaining their approval. It takes extra money to buy 'green' or biological or durable. Deep down I fear to trust and I hold on to control mechanisms, while practicing a humble and modest attitude and learning about my limitations and potential. Authenticity is an inner state of another (=free and serving) mind, directed by faith and the eternal promise that whatever happens, I am loved by the Creator and therefore things will turn out to be ... just fine'.

As I need others to look at me, also organizations and institutions need an outsider or follower to regularly check and judge their level of Corporate Authenticity. My checklists register policies, value definitions and concrete, practical measures on all business levels, as well as defining the so-called corporate personality.

It's a kind of corporate psychological assessment. Customers, employees and relations will appreciate an assessed Authentic Company. Imagine an authentic and non authentic company offering the same kind of product or service... which one gets your money?'

Authentic followership is about how employees or customers follow the leaders (and organizations) for authentic reasons (and have an authentic relationship with them). They follow not because they are forced to by coercion, pressure, or personal rewards but because they share the same values, beliefs and convictions. Additionally, authentic followers do not follow blindly or because they fall for an illusion. They have a realistic view of the CEO's/leader's strengths and weaknesses and have an independent judgment. Finally, authentic followers will authenticate the leader. This implies that a follower accepts the claim for leadership from the leader, because the followers have deep held values and convictions, rather than desire for personal power, benefits, or status. Moreover, they judge the behavior of the leader as in congruence with their own beliefs, values and convictions (Shamir & Eilam, 2005).

Walumba c.s. (2008) indicate that the follower perception of the leaders' authenticity was positively related to individual follower job satisfaction and job performance. This will benefit customers or buyers as well.

13.

Inspiration & Sources

All the inspiration is from personal experience, knowledge and beliefs combined with online studies of articles and texts (in no particular order):

1. zbc.nu/main.asp?ChapterID=4504apple.com/nl
2. leadership-training.suite101.com/article.cfm/authentic_corporate_culture
3. radian6.com/applications/360-degrees-of-your-brand
4. imediaconnection.com/content/7332.asp
5. jshueywa.blogspot.com/2009/01/corporate-authenticity-and-role-of.html
6. socialmediatoday.com/SMC/70259
7. nl.wikipedia.org/wiki/Experiment_van_Milgram
8. authenticbusiness.co.uk/archive/directory.aspx?classid=115
9. managementhelp.org/prsn_wll/authentc.htm
10. toth.ro/identity.htm
11. kentmkeith.com/
12. brandchannel.com/papers_review.asp?sp_id=1360
13. blog.marketingdoctor.tv
14. zorgmarketingplatform.nl/page/226/zorgmarketing-praktijkvoorbeelden-cases.html
15. zbc.nu/main.asp?ChapterID=2918
16. beyondintractability.org/essay/trust_building

17. howtodothings.com/business/how-to-build-business-credibility
18. positiveenergy.info/YellowBrickRoad_Summary.pdf
19. essentialism.net/individual_valuism.htm
20. hartenziel.nl/artikel/De_kracht_van_hoop
21. homepages.luc.edu/~dschwei/economicdemocracy.htm
22. ecosystemvaluation.org/big_picture.htm
23. ratical.com/many_worlds/seeingPCW.html
24. contrahour.com/contrahour/martin-armstrong
25. pragmaticmarketing.com/publications/magazine/8/1/re-inventing-product-management-with-love
26. thepublicdiscourse.com/2010/01/1122
27. businessballs.com/love.htm
28. globalmindshift.wordpress.com/being-inclusive
29. authentic.gilbert.org
30. barnesandnoble.com/Handbook-of-Hope/C-Richard-Snyder/e/9780126540505
31. leadership-training.suite101.com/article.cfm/authentic_corporate_culture
32. valuebasedmanagement.net
33. time.com/time/specials/2007/article/0,28804,1720049_1720050_1722070-2,00.html - ixzz0j17WQzMU
34. communicatieonline.nl/nieuws/bericht/sociaal-wordt-het-nieuwe-statussymbool
35. marketing.about.com/od/marketingyourbrand/a/internalbrand.htm
36. psychologytoday.com/basics/happiness
37. positivesharing.com/category/happy-companies
38. authenticitybook.com/book
39. hbswk.hbs.edu/archive/3684.html
40. twynstragudde.nl/tg.htm?id=5462
41. burnin.nl/?id=div_art_hrs
42. talentwijs.com/Site/weetjes/Artikelen/2009/11/25_Dienend_leiderschap.html
43. mvonederland.nl/degrotemvobibliotheek/publicaties/8706
44. springerlink.com/content/y11253811n627w73
45. methodproducts.co.uk/assets/method_humanifesto.pdf
46. total-performance-scorecard.com
47. billgeorge.org/page/the-new-leaders-collaborative-not-commanding

48. changingminds.org/principles/authority.htm
49. aaa-triplea.org/spiritueel_management.html
50. trainingpd.suite101.com/article.cfm/change_management_and_innovation
51. suite101.com/blog/joni188/leadership_best_practices - ixzz0jeVGKM3N
52. markensteijn.com/kwetsbaarheid.htm
53. 12manage.com/methods_greenleaf_servant_leadership.html
54. primestrategies.com/newsletter/archives/appreciation
55. presence.net
56. solonline.org/presencing
57. greenleaf.org/whatissl/
58. managementlab.org
59. fsw.vu.nl/nl/studenten/masteropleidingen/beleid-communicatie-en-organisatie/afstudeeropdrachten/leiderschap-in-organisaties.asp
60. learnthis.ca/2009/08/do-you-demonstrate-moral-leadership
61. eve-olution.net/home/index.asp
62. pewsocialtrends.org/pubs/708/gender-leadership
63. volkskrant.nl/archief_gratis/article900359.ece/Soms_een_man,_soms_een_vrouw_als_leider
64. compadres.nl/welkom/index.php?option=com_content&view=article&id=540:het-onbehagen-van-de-man&catid=46:boeken&Itemid=118
65. bizjournals.com/pittsburgh/stories/2003/05/05/smallb2.html
66. slideshare.net/bossch00/marketing-moet-zichzelf-opnieuw-uitvinden-tex-gunning
67. cognitieve-evolutie.nl/index
68. wikipedia.org/wiki/Reputatie
69. brainyquote.com/
70. groenportaal.nl/nieuws/200801/hoe_oliebedrijven_werken_aan_een_duurzame_reputatie_5194.shtml
71. ccat.sas.upenn.edu/~haroldfs/popcult/handouts/authentic.html
72. thetruthseeker.co.uk/article.asp?ID=185
73. themanager.org/Marketing/Customer_Perception.htm
74. wikipedia.org/wiki/Authenticity_(philosophy)
75. wikipedia.org/wiki/Morality
76. wikipedia.org/wiki/Integrity
77. wikipedia.org/wiki/Credibility amm

78. librarything.nl/tag/communication:://www.rickross.com/reference/brainwashing/brainwashing20.html
79. existential-therapy.com/General_Overview.htm
80. webanalisten.nl/analyse/de-6-geheimen-van-verleiding.html
81. psychowerk.com/adviseur/adviseur_bestanden/page0518.htm
82. skepp.be/artikels/debat/debattechnieken-van-pseudo-wetenschappers/hoe-moet-je-argumenteren-met-paras-en-pseud
83. jshueywa.blogspot.com/2009/01/corporate-authenticity-and-role-of.html
84. cohttp://skepp.be/search/node/Palmarinignitieve-evolutie.nl/index/emoties-versus-gevoelens
85. quotegarden.com/
86. coolquotes.com/
87. getrichslowly.org/blog/2008/08/25/the-psychology-of-happiness-13-steps-to-a-better-life/
88. ezinearticles.com/?10-Ways-To-Bring-More-Happiness-Into-Your-Life&id=367756
89. dealerinfo.nl/2004/411/manage.htm
90. ugent.be/nl/nieuwsagenda/nieuws/vyncke.htm
91. integro-inc.com/volume1.htm
92. total-performance-scorecard.com/p_overview.php
93. rickross.com/reference/brainwashing/brainwashing20.html
94. cognitieve-evolutie.nl/index/emoties-versus-gevoelens
95. themanager.org/Marketing/Customer_Perception.htm
96. humsyn.be/OCI%20PIF%20NL.pdf
97. spiritus-temporis.com/generation-z/
98. questia.com/googleScholar
99. en.wikipedia.org/wiki/Generation_Y
100. businessissues.nl/?ContentID=3030#Bladwijzer7
101. express.be/business/nl/management
102. contextualpsychology.org/the_pursuit_of_happiness
103. abcnews.go.com/Business/economists-warn-financial-us-economy/story?id=9990828
104. goldenjackass.com/main5.html
105. windmillministries.org/frames/NL-CH18A.htm
106. trendsresearch.com/forecast.html
107. jsmineset.com

108. mediapost.com/publications/?fa=Articles.showArticle&art_aid =117011
109. edelman.com/news/ShowOne.asp?ID=222
110. yalom.com/gift/intro
111. quotationspage.com/
112. luc.edu/faculty/dschwei/NewCapNewWorld.WW.pdf
113. counterpunch.com/whitney04162010.html
114. pluspost.nl/henk-kraaijenhof-verklaart-de-cultuur-van-de – angst/28869
115. financialsense.com
116. pcdf.org/2000/The%20Mindful%20Market.htm
117. marketoracle.co.uk/
118. wisdomquotes.com/
119. fredrickson.socialpsychology.org/
120. nl.wikipedia.org/wiki/Hoop
121. sustainability-index.com/07_htmle/sustainability/corpsustainability.html
122. wanttoknow.info/youweremadeforthis

14.

Quotes

1. Pg 10: Learning without reflection is a waste, reflection without learning is dangerous (Confucius)
2. Pg 11: There's nothing like rejection, to make you do an inventory of yourself (James L Burke)
3. Pg 13: A new time, a new misison: Act Locally - Think Community (Pleu)
4. Pg 14: When a government is dependent upon bankers for money, they and not the leaders of the government control the situation, since the hand that gives is above the hand that takes. Money has no motherland; financiers are without patriotism and without decency; their sole object is gain (Napoleon Bonaparte).
5. Pg 16: Politics is supposed to be the second-oldest profession. I have come to realize that it bears a very close resemblance to the first (Ronald Reagan)
6. Pg 16:In the counsels of Government, we must guard against the acquisition of unwarranted influence, whether sought or unsought, by the Military Industrial Complex. The potential for the disastrous rise of misplaced power exists, and will persist. We must never let the weight of this combination endanger our

liberties of democratic processes. We should take nothing for granted. Only an alert and knowledgeable citizenry can compel the proper meshing of the huge industrial and military machinery of defence with our peaceful methods and goals, so that security and liberty may prosper together.(Eisenhower, farewell speech 1961).

7. Pg 17: You can have power over people as long as you don't take everything away from them. But when you've robbed a man of everything, he's no longer in your power (A. Solzhenitsyn)

8. Pg 19: The very word "secrecy" is repugnant in a free and open society; and we are as a people inherently and historically opposed to secret societies, to secret oaths and to secret proceedings. We decided long ago that the dangers of excessive and unwarranted concealment of pertinent facts far outweighed the dangers, which are cited to justify it. Even today, there is little value in opposing the threat of a closed society by imitating its arbitrary restrictions. Even today, there is little value in insuring the survival of our nation if our traditions do not survive with it. And there is very grave danger that an announced need for increased security will be seized upon by those anxious to expand its meaning to the very limits of official censorship and concealment. That I do not intend to permit to the extent that it is in my control (JF Kennedy) ."

9. Pg 20: There are three ways of dealing with difference: domination, compromise, and integration. By domination only one side gets what it wants; by compromise neither side gets what it wants; by integration we find a way by which both sides may get what they wish (Mary Parker Follett)

10. Pg 21: It takes a lot of courage to release the familiar and seemingly secure, to embrace the new. But there is no real security in what is no longer meaningful (Alan Cohen)

11. Pg 23: When you come to the end of your rope, tie a knot and hang on (FD Roosevelt)
12. Pg 24: To acquire knowledge, one must study; but to acquire wisdom, one must observe (Marylin vos Savant)
13. Pg 25: Je wensen zijn een voorgevoel van dat wat je daadwerkelijk kunt bereiken (Goethe)".
14. Pg 29: Every time we choose safety, we reinforce fear (Cheri Huber).
15. Pg 30: If you are distressed by anything external, the pain is not due to the thing itself, but to your estimate of it; and this you have the power to revoke at any moment (Marcus Aurelius).
16. Pg 31: Problems cannot be solved by the same level of thinking that created them (Einstein).
17. Pg 32: Too many people are thinking of security instead of opportunity. They seem to be more afraid of life than death (James Bymes)
18. Pg 33: The best thing about the future is that it only comes one day at a time (Abraham Lincoln).
19. Pg 39: Showing bravery and compassion is an act of integrity and of the highest significance. (Clarissa Estes).
20. Pg 42: Daring to recognize dependencr, is the beginning of autonomy (Pleu)
21. Pg 47: If there is to be a human future, we must bring ourselves into balanced relationship with one another and the Earth. This requires building economies with heart (David Korten) .
22. Pg 49: Sometimes something has got to happen first, before something happens (J. Cruijff)
23.   Pg 50: Where there is no vision, there is no hope (George Washington Carver)
24. Pg 52: The torture of a bad conscience is the hell of a living soul (John Calvijn).

25. Pg 53: When things are bad, we take comfort in the thought that they could always be worse. And when they are, we find hope in the thought that things are so bad they have to get better (unknown)
26. Pg 57: If we stop blaming others, we especially discover out amazing self (Pleu)
27. Pg 59: There is no true faith possible without deeds to bring the believed desire nearer (Pleu).
28. Pg 60: Hope sees the invisible, feels the intangible and achieves the impossible (Unknown)
29. Pg 61: Blessed are those, who do not see and still believe. (Johannes 20:29 NT)
30. Pg 64: Trust is the currency of the new world (Steven Covey).
31. Pg 64: Trust is a peculiar resource; it is built rather than depleted by use (Unknown)
32. Pg 65: Trust means renunciatoon control and is in fact giving the other the opportunity to do what must be done, trusting it will not be abused.(Paul Schnabel).
33. Pg 67: Everything that irritates us about others can lead us to an understanding about ourselves (Carl Jung).
34. Pg 71: There is always a way to be honest without being brutal (Arthur Dobrin).
35. Pg 77: Het is niet voldoende om te weten wat goed is; je moet het ook kunnen doen (George Bernard Shaw)
36. Pg 73: Sure, winning trust is an heroic act: you need to conquer yourself and take the risk that others violate that given trust. Trust is therefore an utterly humane but dangerous merit. (Gerard Bodifée)
37. Pg 78: The companies that survive longest are the one's that work out what they uniquely can give to the world not just growth or money but their excellence, their respect for others, or their ability to make people happy. Some call those things a soul (Charles Handy)

38. Pg 82: Only strength can cooperate. Weakness can only beg (Dwight D. Eisenhower)
39. Pg 84: If you want to be incrementally better: Be competitive. If you want to be exponentially better: Be cooperative (unknown).
40. Pg 85: If you want to build a ship, don't herd people together to collect wood and don't assign them tasks and work, but rather teach them to long for the endless immensity of the sea (Antoine de Saint-Exupéry).
41. Pg 89: The more you are willing to accept responsibility for your actions, the more credibility you will have (Brian Koslow).
42. Pg 90: Credibility is like virginity. Once you lose it, you can never get it back (Unknown)
43. Pg 91: Selfishness is not living as one wishes to live, it is asking others to live as one wishes to live (Oscar Wild)
44. Pg 96: Try not to become a man of success but rather try to become a man of value (Albert Einstein)
45. Pg 96: Attitude is a little thing that makes a big difference (Winston Churchill)
46. Pg 101: Love all, trust a few, do wrong to none (W.Shakespeare)
47. Pg 102: It is hard to believe that a man is telling the truth when you know that you would lie if you were in his place (H.L. Mencke)
48. Pg 103: All credibility, all good conscience, all evidence of truth come only from the senses (Friedrich Nietzsche)
49. Pg 103: Sometimes I wonder whether the world is being run by smart people who are putting us on, or by imbeciles who really mean it (Mark Twain).
50. Pg 106: Leaders have now invented 'preventive warfare'. We are now starting a ME war, in order to prevent a possible war. We now sow death, in order to forestall death. (Jan Marijnissen)

51. Pg 109: I know you're out there. I know that you're afraid. you're afraid of change. I don't know the future. didn't come here to tell you how this is going to end. I came here to tell you how it's going to begin. I'm going to show a world without rules and controls, without borders or boundaries. A world where anything is possible. Where we go from there is a choice I leave to you (Matrix movie).
52. Pg 110: Christianity is the companion of liberty in all its conflicts – the cradle of its infancy, and the divine source of its claims (Alexis Detocqueville).
53. Pg 111: If you limit your choices only to what seems possible or reasonable, you disconnect yourself from what you truly want, and all that is left is compromise (Robert Fritz).
54. Pg 113: The reward for conformity is that everyone likes you, but yourself (Rita Mae Brown)
55. Pg 113: I'am convinced that being authentic brings a major benefit: you feel better recognized for what you are … a unique personality. That's rather a rewarding response. Isn't it? Now, how would that work out on a corporate level? It's the same! (Pleu)
56. Pg 114: How does one become a butterfly?" she asked. You must want to fly so much that you are willing to give up being a caterpillar (unknown).
57. Pg 116: Don't listen to "It's not done that way." Maybe it's not, but maybe you will. Don't listen to "You're taking too big a chance." Michelangelo would not have painted the Sistine chapel. Above all: don't listen when the little voice of fear inside says, "They're all smarter than you out there. They're more talented, they're taller, smarter, prettier, luckier and have connections…". If you follow a path that interests you, not to the exclusion of love, sensitivity and cooperation, but with the strength of conviction that you can move others by your own

efforts. Do not make success or failure the criteria. The chances are you'll be a person worthy of your own respect (Neil Simon)
58. Pg 116: What we really want to do is what we are really meant to do. When we do what we are meant to do, money comes to us, doors open for us, we feel useful, and the work we do feels like play to us (Julia Cameron).
59. Pg 117: The beginning of thought is in disagreement, not only with others but also with ourselves (Eric Hoffer).
60. Pg 118: Once the fight is finally understood, wonders are possible (Mao).
61. Pg 122: Classic economic theory, based as it is on an inadequate theory of human motivation, could be revolutionized by accepting the reality of higher human needs, including the impulse to self actualization and the love for the highest values (Abraham Maslow)
62. Pg 124: If the only tool you have is a hammer, you tend to see every problem as a nail (Maslow)
63. Pg 127: You see things; and you say, "Why?" But I dream things that never were; and I say, "Why not? (Bernard Shaw)
64. Pg 130: Each generation imagines itself to be more intelligent than the one that went before it, and wiser than the one that comes after it (George Orwell)
65. Pg 131: If everything seems under control, you're just not going fast enough (Mario Andretti)
66. Pg 132: Unless commitment is made, there are only promises and hopes; but no plans (Peter F. Drucker)
67. Pg 135: Finally, brothers, whatever is true, whatever is noble, whatever is right, whatever is pure, whatever is lovely, whatever is admirable-if anything is excellent or praiseworthy-think about such things (Jesus).
68. Pg 139: Coming together is a beginning. Keeping together is progress. Working together is success (Henry Ford).□

69. Pg 143: I don't know what your destiny will be, but one thing I do know: the only ones among you who will be really happy are those who have sought and found how to serve (Albert Schweitzer).
70. Pg 146: Gratitude is not only the greatest of virtues, but the parent of all the others (Cicero) .
71. Pg 147: Optimism is the faith that leads to achievement. Nothing can be done without hope and confidence (Helen Keller)
72. Pg 148: When I were a child, I spoke like a child, thought like a child and reasoned like a child, but when I became a grown-up, I abandoned everything I considered childish. (Apostle Paul, NT)
73. Pg 150: The most important ingredient we put into any relationship is not what we say or what we do, but what we are (S.R. Covey)
74. Pg 151: Don't be humble. You aren't that great (Golda Meir)
75. Pg 169 De enige échte ontdekkingsreis bestaat niet in het zoeken van nieuwe landschappen, maar in het ontvangen van nieuwe ogen (Marcel Proust)
76. Pg 154: Presence is more than just being there (M.Forbes)
77. Pg 154: Now we see things imperfectly, like puzzling reflections in a mirror, but then we will see everything with perfect clarity. All that I know now is partial and incomplete, but then I will know everything completely, just as God now knows me completely (Aposte Paul, NT)
78. Pg 156: You have to leave the city of your comfort and go into the wilderness of your intuition. What you'll discover will be wonderful. What you'll discover is yourself (Alan Alda).
79. Pg 158: How wonderful it is that nobody need wait a single moment before starting to improve the world (Anne Frank).
80. Pg 160: The trouble with having an open mind, of course, is that people will insist on coming along and trying to put things in it (Terry Pratchett)

81. Pg 162: Appreciation is a wonderful thing: It makes what is excellent in others belong to us as well (Voltaire)
82. Pg 164: Synchronicity reveals the meaningful connections between the subjective and objective world (Carl G. Jung)
83. Pg 165: We cannot let another person into our hearts or minds unless we empty ourselves. We can truly listen to him or truly hear her only out of emptiness (M Scott Peck)
84. Pg 166: The fact that man knows right from wrong proves his intel-lectual superiority to other creatures; but the fact that he can do wrong proves his moral inferiority to any creature that cannot (Mark Twain)
85. Pg 167:Diegenen die je dient, groeien die als persoon, worden ze zelfbewuster, gezonder, wijzer, vrijer, zelfstandiger en ontwikkelen ze zich zo, dat ze ook dienstbaar willen worden? (R. Greanleaf)
86. Pg 170: So God created man in his own image, in the image of God he created him; male and female he created them (Genesis)
87. Pg 172: All great men are gifted with intuition. They know without reasoning or analysis, what they need to know (Alexis Carrel).
88. Pg 173: We encounter spiritual issues every time we wonder where the universe comes from, why we are here, or what happens when we die. We also become spiritual when we become moved by values such as beauty, love, or creativity that seem to reveal a meaning or power beyond our visible world. An idea or practice is "spiritual" when it reveals our personal desire to establish a felt-relationship with the deepest meanings or powers governing life (Robert C Fuller).
89. Pg 175: Neither shall they say, See here! or, see there! for, behold, the kingdom of God is within you (Jesus, Luke 17).
90. Pg 176: What the heart gives away is never gone ...It is kept in the hearts of others (Robin St. John)

91. Pg 177: Coaching is unlocking a person's potential to maximize their own performance. It is helping them to learn rather than teaching them (Timothy Gallwey).
92. Pg 178: Your vision will become clear only when you can look into your own heart. Who looks outside, dreams; who looks inside, awakens (Carl Jung)
93. Pg 180: Self-expression must pass into communication for its fulfillment (Pearl S. Buck).
94. Pg 181: Our chief want in life is someone who will make us do what we can (Emerson)
95. Pg 181: Have the courage to say no. Have the courage to face the truth. Do the right thing because it is right. Theses are the magic keys to living your life with integrity (W. Clement Stone)
96. Pg 182: Half of the work that is done in this world is to make things appear what they are not (E. R. Beadle)
97. Pg 184: The truth is more important than the facts (F.L. Wright
98. Pg 186: The basic tool for the manipulation of reality is the manipulation of words. If you can control the meaning of words, you can control the people who must use the words (Ph. K. Dick)
99. Pg 186: The difference between fiction and reality is that fiction has to make sense (Tom Clancy)
100. Pg 188: The shortest and surest way to live with honor in the world is to be in reality what we would appear to be (Socrates)
101. Pg 189: Authenticiteit is het belangrijkste dat je reputatie bepaalt (Cees van Riel).
102. Pg 189: Executive's good intentions and words, like their compa-nies' stocks, lose their value when nothing backs them up (AWatts)
103. Pg 191: To separate the purpose of a business from the purpose of people who are in the business is, I think, not a good thing (Michael Josephson)

104. Pg 191: Life is the continuous adjustment of internal relations to external relations (Herbert Spencer)
105. Pg 193: The leader for today and the future will be focused on how to be, how to develop quality, character, mind-set, values, principles and courage (Frances Hesselbein)
106. Pg 194: When one is out of touch with oneself, one cannot touch others (Anne Morrow Lindbergh).
107. Pg 195: Trickery and treachery are the practices of fools that have not the wits enough to be honest (Benjamin Franklin)
108. Pg 196: Leadership is based on inspiration, not domination; on cooperation, not intimidation (William Arthur Ward)
109. Pg 197: Every man has three characters – that which he exhibits, that which he has, and that which he thinks he has (Karr)
110. Pg 198: Just get rid of the false and you will automatically realize the true (Ho-Shan)
111. Pg 199: If we attach more importance to what other people believe than to what we know to be true - if we value belonging over being - we will not attain authenticity (Nathaniel Branden).
112. Pg 205: Becoming personally convinced of something, is more difficult than trying to prove something scientifically (Peter Leuhof or: Pleu)

www.ingramcontent.com/pod-product-compliance
Ingram Content Group UK Ltd.
Pitfield, Milton Keynes, MK11 3LW, UK
UKHW021319180426
11947UKWH00015B/1319